Thomas George Bonney

Christian Doctrines and Modern Thought

Thomas George Bonney

Christian Doctrines and Modern Thought

ISBN/EAN: 9783337166823

Printed in Europe, USA, Canada, Australia, Japan

Cover: Foto ©Lupo / pixelio.de

More available books at **www.hansebooks.com**

CHRISTIAN DOCTRINES

AND

MODERN THOUGHT

THE BOYLE LECTURES FOR 1891

BY

T. G. BONNEY, D. Sc.

LL.D., F.R.S., F.S.A., F.G.S.

FELLOW OF ST. JOHN'S COLLEGE, CAMBRIDGE, HONORARY CANON OF MANCHESTER
AND EXAMINING CHAPLAIN TO ~~THE LORD~~ BISHOP OF MANCHESTER

LONDON

LONGMANS, GREEN, & CO.

AND NEW YORK: 15 EAST 16th STREET

1892

PREFACE.

KNOWLEDGE has grown from more to more during the present century. It is sometimes tacitly assumed that this advance has been adverse to all definite or systematic theology. In a certain sense this is true. A scientific education develops a habit of mind which is sceptical, in the better sense of the word. By it men are rendered less prone to accept, unless good reason can be shown, either the *ipse dixit* of a teacher or the decree of an assembly; they are led to assign a lower value to ceremonial ordinances and the machinery of an ecclesiastical system; they are more fully convinced of the inadequacy of the human mind to comprehend, and of human words to express, the

b

things which belong, not to the phenomenal and the temporal, but to the unseen and the eternal.

Men thus trained are slow to admit a finality in any expression of truth. To them a creed or a decree of a council represents no more than the nearest approximation to the expression of a thought which could be made by the best qualified judges at that epoch. But since changes take place in the meaning of words, these formulæ may become inadequate or even misleading. Moreover, since the minds of men are modified by education, in the wide sense of the term, their habits of thought are changed; thus, in the process of time, some difficulties are smoothed away, but others may be created. An argument which in one age was convincing, in another may fail to satisfy; while, as a compensation, it is possible to appeal to new facts and to new considerations. In theology, as in war, certain methods of defence and certain weapons of attack become antiquated. At the present day the bravest troops which ever went to battle would be massacred by men of inferior physique and tactical skill, did they take the field with the muskets and artillery which did such good service at Waterloo. In this age, though we may not be superior to our forefathers in dialectics or metaphysics, we have obtained a far more comprehensive view of the natural world, and a closer insight into its processes of operation. By these our position has been materially altered. They have, in a sense, brought men nearer to God by indicating a latent unity in the varied phenomena of the universe, and suggesting that these proceed from and are the outcome of One Almighty Power. But, at the same time, this advance renders our conceptions of that Power less definite. As our conviction of the omnipresence and omnipotence of God grows stronger, our ideas of Him become less anthropomorphic, less capable of expression in words—in short, less definite. Still they are not on this account necessarily less assured. A child's conception of something which is external to himself and partially beyond his experience is frequently clear and definite, but it is also, as a necessary consequence, inadequate or even incorrect. When he has grown to manhood, it may become much more vague, but at the same time may be a much nearer approximation to the truth.

A change of this kind is taking place in the sphere of religious thought. Phrases which formerly satisfied are now felt to be inadequate; arguments once deemed conclusive now fail to convince—nay, in some cases, if resorted to, would produce the opposite effect. The progress of knowledge, even during the past half-century, the discoveries in geology, biology, archæology, and philology, have compelled theologians to modify their views as to the nature and function of inspiration, and the date, the origin, and the authority, historic or scientific, of some portions of the Bible. Views are commonly held and expressed by men of approved orthodoxy for which, five and twenty years ago, they would have been denounced as heretics and infidels. Science is now free to investigate the early history of our race, and to interpret the picture-writing of the Book of Nature as best she can, without being under any obligation to force the results into conformity with the narrative in the Book of Genesis, or with references to the same in later parts of the Scriptures. Only those who can remember something of the old days, who have themselves heard the thumping of the drum ecclesiastic, and felt a little of the storm of theological vituperation, can appreciate the blessings of the present freedom. But a price has to be paid—as it always must be—for this rapid advance. Liberty, quickly won after long thraldom, is liable to be misused, and some persons now imagine that in the process of clearing

away parasitic growths and accumulated encum-
brances the tower of our strength has been shaken,
and that Christianity in future must be counted
among the "creeds outworn."

With some of the difficulties, of which we now
hear much, I endeavoured to deal in an earlier
course of lectures;[1] but, as it seemed to me, another
aspect of them still called for consideration. It is
this. Supposing we are convinced, not only that
a revelation is possible, but also that one has been
made in the Person of Christ—supposing, in a
word, we believe the Scriptures of the New Testament, can we also accept the theological dogmas
on which the various branches of the Catholic
Church are generally agreed? In the doctrinal
statements of the New Testament there is usually
no attempt at elaborate definition or minute
precision, but during the controversies which dis-

[1] The Boyle Lectures for 1890, published in "Old Truths in
Modern Lights."

turbed the earlier centuries of Christianity these statements were subjected to deductive treatment, and the results were sanctioned by authority. How far, then, has this dogmatic theology, a system which has been the outcome of some centuries of speculation and conflict, been affected by the increase in our knowledge and the changes in our methods of thought?

I determined, therefore—though conscious of many deficiencies—to attempt an answer to this question; to examine some of the leading statements in Christian doctrine or dogma,[1] in order to see whether, as students of modern science, we could still accept and remain satisfied with these as the best approximations to the expression of mysteries which in themselves transcend human understanding and language.

In this attempt I am not concerned, since I am

---

[1] Between the one and the other no hard-and-fast line can be drawn, since the dogmas of councils depend for their validity upon the doctrines of inspired teachers.

a member of the Church of England, to discuss dogmas which she does not accept, or to hold a brief for any other branch of the Church. It is enough for me if it can be shown that the expressions in her authorized formulæ are not out of harmony with the conclusions to which we are led by modern science.

Neither do I feel myself bound by the dominant and popular views at this or at any other age of the Church. I am fully aware that some of the opinions expressed in the last two lectures will be at present unacceptable to many—perhaps to a majority—of the members (at any rate, clerical) of the Church of England. But I have lived long enough (as I have already intimated) to see opinions once loudly denounced become generally accepted, and the men, who were esteemed by one generation as champions of orthodoxy, regarded by the next as little better than theological knights of La Mancha. Hence I care little so long as I do not transgress the limits of opinion which are laid down by the Church of which I am a member; and if that which appears to my mind a truth be unpopular, I remember the lesson taught in the old saying, "It moves for all that!"

The method of treatment which has been adopted is necessarily one-sided. Some readers may be surprised at finding that, practically, no reference is made to the writings of eminent theologians, whether of the earlier or the later age of Church history. This is done, not because I am ignorant of what has been written—though I have never made a special study of dogmatic theology—but because the point of view adopted in these lectures has excluded any particular reference for purposes of argument to authorities anterior to the present age. It has been my endeavour to look at the questions, if possible, from the standpoint not of an ecclesiastic but of a layman who was generally acquainted with the results of modern science, who had become familiar with its methods by the careful study of one of its branches, and who was beginning to feel uneasy whether he might not be compelled to quit the communion of the Church of England for one of simpler creed and vaguer definitions, could such be found.

How imperfectly this design has been executed, no one can feel more deeply than myself. Each subject is so vast that the compass of a single lecture is utterly inadequate for its treatment. The time which, in a life burdened, as is mine, with many inevitable duties and engagements, could be devoted to thought and study for this special purpose, was wholly insufficient. But, inasmuch as at the present day very few of the clergy of the Church of England can also be numbered among the active students of Natural Science, there may be something novel—if there is nothing else—in the point of view which has been taken in these lectures. I can only hope that my incomplete and, as I fear, occasionally rather disjointed thoughts may allay mental disquiet in some, and suggest ideas to others which may ultimately bear good fruit. If only they convince a few earnest seekers after truth that Christianity is not to be reckoned among the illusions of humanity; that faith may grow stronger in the process of putting away childish things and of breaking the leading-strings which have been twined and fitted by the hands of man: that the same light shines from Nature and from Revelation, they will have served their purpose. Speaking for myself, I have been led by science to abandon some of the notions which I was taught when a child; to alienate myself from, and oppose, a party in our Church towards which, as a young man, I had a strong leaning; but this mental change has added a fresh consecration to the earth, to the study of Nature, and to the whole work of life, by showing that all comes from God, and all can lead to God.

T. G. BONNEY.

SUMMARY OF THE LECTURES.[1]

LECTURE I. THE LOGOS (WORD).

LECTURE II. THE HOLY SPIRIT.

---

[1] The Boyle Lectures were formerly delivered in the Chapel Royal, Whitehall; but as that ceased to be used for Divine service in the summer of 1890, the present course was given, by the kind permission of the Rev. Harry Jones, at a special afternoon service in the church of St. Philip and St. James, Regent Street.

LECTURE III. THE HOLY TRINITY.

LECTURE IV. THE INCARNATION.

LECTURE V. THE ATONEMENT.

LECTURE VI. THE RESURRECTION.

LECTURE VII. THE SACRAMENTS.

LECTURE VIII.   THE CHURCH.

LECTURE I.

THE WORD.

"In the beginning was the Word, and the Word was with God, and the Word was God. . . . All things were made by Him; and without Him was not anything made that was made."— St. John i. 1, 3.

ANOTHER century is approaching its end. It has been characterized by mental activity, exceptional in its amount and very diverse in its manifestations. During this epoch, which indeed began rather more than a hundred years ago, the mechanical arts have attained to a wonderful perfection, and thus, directly and indirectly the instruments of scientific research, the methods of investigation have become more refined and more precise. Hence vast stores of exact knowledge have been accumulated; results of more or less exact induction are abundant.

B

How do these affect our position as Christians? Has this been rendered more reasonable or less reasonable by the advance in science, the progress of knowledge? Is it still possible—nay, easy—to be not only a sincere believer in Christianity, but also an honest man of science? Are we now more exposed than formerly to charges of mental inconsistency? Are we now involved in graver difficulties than have always attended the acceptance of any form of theism, which applies to God the attributes of personality?

We must not expect, I warn you, a direct reply to these questions. There are difficulties which are inherent; which always have existed, and, so far as we can see, always will exist. We must be satisfied if we find that the number of these has been reduced rather than augmented, and the issue narrowed and simplified in aspect.

Christian doctrines—I refer to those admitted, practically by every branch of the Church, to be of cardinal importance, and to the simpler sense of these—present us with difficulties which may be distinguished as physical and metaphysical, as belonging to the region of sensible existences and to that of mental concepts. Of these, the latter, for a long time, have not undergone, so far as I can see, any very important change. Alterations are in form rather than in nature. The old questions, the old perplexities, the old arguments reappear in modern phrase. Not a few of these are more ancient than Christianity, and belong to monotheism, if not to theism itself; others, if slightly later in date than the rise of Christianity, are independent in origin. In the works of Philo, and Plutarch, and Epictetus, not to mention others, we not seldom find speculations, arguments, and conclusions as to the Divine nature and its relations with the universe, which might be accepted gladly by Christians.

In the region of abstract thought the mind of man appears to have reached, at a comparatively early period, the limits to which it could attain. It has even been asserted that no real advance has been made since the age of Plato. Be that as it may, there are some grounds for maintaining that in this region practically everything has been done which is within the range of the calculus (to use a mathematical phrase) at our disposal. If, then, any further advance is possible, it must be in the modification of the symbols employed or in our knowledge of nature and of the relations of the concrete, upon which these symbols depend. It will be some gain to have recognized clearly the essential difference between concept and actuality, between word and thing; for the confusion of their provinces, the obliteration of the boundary between the physical and the metaphysical, has been a fruitful source of difficulties in the past; especially when it is forgotten that the connotation of a word, commonly employed in the one sphere, cannot remain wholly unchanged when it is transferred to the other.

We must not expect that all difficulties will vanish. How can this be when they have their origin in the nature of things, and must be created whenever the finite attempts to comprehend and define the Infinite ? But they may prove to have been diminished rather than increased by recent progress in inductive knowledge. We may find that we have now to encounter, not a crowd, collectively numerous, even if not always individually formidable, but one or two difficulties which are clearly defined, and prove to be the inevitable results of the conditions of the present life. We must admit that we have to make some assumptions, but these are few instead of many ; they are at the outset, not at every stage ; while the methods of reasoning which result from scientific investigation can be employed in obtaining indirect confirmation of the validity of our initial hypotheses.

I do not propose to consider the effect of scientific progress on the belief in a God. The latter, even in its most perfected aspect, is not characteristic of Christianity alone. The thoughtful Jew, to name none other, had attained, it matters not how for our present purpose, to monotheism. But the theology of the Christian is separated by distinctive characteristics from the theologies of most Oriental

nations, while in some respects it occupies an
intermediate position. They have diverged in one
of two opposite directions. Either they have
pushed the monistic idea so far as to affirm not
only that God is source and author of everything,
but also the converse proposition, that everything
which exists is God—that is, they have strayed
into pantheism—or, by maintaining an eternal
distinction of opposites in the Divine principle
they have been led into Manichæan dualism, or
some form of polytheism.

Christianity differs from Judaism and other
forms of monotheism in its assertion of the Trini-
tarian doctrine; thereby indicating an approach to
the principle of distinction which has just been
named. Thus, during the earlier stages of its
history, it obviously oscillated between an absolute
monotheism and some limited form of polytheism.
Gnostic philosophy is the record of a constant
struggle to reconcile the monistic and dualistic
ideas. It led back, almost invariably, however
ingeniously the fact might be concealed, to the

polytheism which it professed to have abandoned, and on this account mainly was so strenuously resisted by the Church. Though at one time only a single letter seemed to divide the two great parties, the Arians and the Orthodox, they were in reality sundered by a hemisphere of theological thought.

In the controversies which agitated the Church from the second to the fifth century, the subject which I am about to consider, the nature and relationship of the Logos, was exceptionally prominent. For our present purpose it is necessary to indicate very briefly the origin and history of the doctrine, so that we may be in a position to see whether it is less congruous with modern than with ancient thought. But I must make two preliminary remarks, lest perchance we should forget their importance. First, that words are only symbols, to express ideas and to facilitate processes of reasoning, and that these abstractions cannot be invested with concrete properties. When we find this done and difficulties conjured up by

the metaphysician's art, we must remember that
they are only cloud phantoms, no more really alive
than a decimal fraction or an elliptic integral.
Secondly, that for these symbols, we have no other
basis than the experience of our senses. Abstract
ideas *may* exist, innate ideas *may* be; this, as it
seems to me, we can neither prove nor disprove:
but we can prove that all those which are employed
in our processes of thought are the results, direct or
indirect, of experience. The only thing, as Descartes
has said, of which I can be absolutely certain is my
own consciousness. The only knowledge which I
can really obtain must be through the evidence of
my senses. Experience, then, is the basis of all our
knowledge, in the strict sense of the word,—it
provides the substratum of all thought. Without
it, so far as we are concerned, thought is no more
possible than is life without matter. This being
so, we must also remember that words, while they
continue in use, may part with some attributes
connoted by them, and acquire others ; may change
by intussusception and excretion, like a living

thing, so that their meaning in the course of centuries is greatly altered.

Here let me ask you to remember that this lecture is part of a series, and not to take offence, if occasionally I may make use of a phrase which would be consistent with Sabellianism or pantheism.

To return, then, to the history of the idea conveyed by the term Logos. We have no precise single equivalent for it in English. It was used in Greek in a variety of senses, at the one extremity being that connoted by *word* (not in the sense of a name or title), at the other that connoted by *reason*. The theological idea which the term Logos is intended to symbolize was not unknown to the Jews. In the Targums, which, though later as documents than the Christian era, embody teaching which is at any rate somewhat earlier than it, " God—not as in His permanent manifestation or manifest presence—but as revealing ‑Himself, is designated *Memra*," [1] which is the Aramaic equiva-

---

[1] Edersheim, "Life and Times of Jesus the Messiah," bk. i. ch. iv. (vol. i. p. 47).

C

lent of Word or Logos. The last term at a still
earlier period had obtained a place in Greek Philosophy. It was employed by each of the two great
schools of thought, the Stoics and the Platonists.
The former regarded reason and force as inherent in
matter, the latter as external to matter. But the
Stoics admitted a certain antithesis in the monistic
conception—the existence of an active and a passive
in the unity of substance. By an extension of this
differentiation these two were conceived as standing
in a relation to each other, somewhat like that
of life and its physical basis,—the passive being
designated ὕλη (material, stuff) the active λόγος.
By some the latter was invested with personality,
and thus an antithesis admitted between matter
and God. But still the two terms of the antithesis
were regarded as "expressing modes of a single
substance, separable in thought and name, but not
in reality."[1] In the dualism of the Platonists
reason and force were held to be external to

[1] Hatch, "The Influence of Greek Ideas and Usages upon the
Christian Church" (Hibbert Lectures, vii. p. 176).

matter. On this God, as it were, operated, following out thoughts which existed in His mind. This
pre-existent Form, Pattern, or Idea, was further
differentiated, and ultimately designated the Logos.
Thus, in the anterior history of this term, as has been
pointed out by Dr. Westcott,[1] there were two conceptions of different origin and different nationality
—the Palestinian (Memra), the *Revealer;* and the
Greek conception, (sides, rather than differences of
which are represented by Stoics and Platonists) the
Reason. These conceptions respectively dominate
in the minds of the two great writers on the subject
in the first century, St. John and Philo ; dominate,
I say ; for in neither writer is the other concept
excluded. To quote a summary of the doctrine of
Philo, he is monistic in teaching " that the world was
made, not by inferior or opposing beings, but by God.
It is the expression of His thought." But in this
thought (here Philo adopts the Platonic doctrine
of Forms) an ideal world had existence before that
the thought went outside God to create the present

[1] " The Gospel according to St. John," Introd. p. xvii.

world.　Thus the Logos represents the reason, will,
or word of God in a special form of its activity.
It is His creative energy.　It is the instrument by
which He made all things.[1]

We see, then, that in the teaching of Philo we
come very near to the doctrine of St. John.　But
there is this difference, that, in the former, the Logos
appears as a part of an elaborate philosophical
system; in the latter, as a bare statement, like
the assertion of an historical fact.　St. John speaks
as one who reveals, not as one who argues.　Like
his Master he teaches as one who has authority,
not as the scribes.　This, then, leads us to one of
the fundamental assumptions of which I spoke.
Christianity, however congruous with reason,
cannot rest on reason alone, because it deals with
a subject which by the nature of the case ultimately
transcends reason.　The latter may indeed lead us
to deem it highly probable that behind phenomena
there is a something yet more real, may enable us

[1]. Hatch, "The Influence of Greek Ideas and Usages upon the
Christian Church" (Hibbert Lectures, vii. pp. 182–187).

by deductive processes to give a philosophic consistency to our hypotheses, but it cannot disclose to us what this is. The " Word " of the Stoics and the Platonists, after all, has only a metaphysical existence; if we claim to have any knowledge which can be called certain, relative though this must always be, we must admit that a revelation from the Divine to the Human is possible. But, as I considered our position in respect to this assumption in a former series of lectures,[1] I will not now dwell further upon it. Admitting, then, that a revelation in the person of Christ and His apostles rests on an assumption, for that is needed to put us in a position to weigh the evidence in its favour, I pass on to see whether it involves us in any new difficulties at the present time.

On the strictly metaphysical side the question remains as it did; but there is another side to the discussion, which, of late years, has been much modified. Those who are familiar with theological

---

[1] These lectures, with some other sermons, are published in a volume entitled "Old Truths in Modern Lights."

speculation, be it Christian or non-Christian, will remember that not a few difficulties have centred on the nature and origin of matter, as to whether it was inseparable from the idea of God or was to be regarded as apart from Him, by whatever process we conceive it called into existence.

In olden time all notions of matter were markedly concrete. Its objectivity was deemed unquestionable ; it was regarded as diverse in form, attributes, and qualities. For long, all advances towards an atomic theory (and this found most favour) by introducing the notion of ultimate indivisibility, gave to matter a very real existence as a popular conception, whatever difficulties there might be in framing a definition. Hence arose ideas of grossness and the like with some, of indestructibility with others—ideas very various and diverse, but not seldom antagonistic to those associated with Divinity. But of late years there has been a remarkable change in opinion, which, however indecisive the results, has certainly dispelled many of the older and grosser conceptions. At the present time, if we are asked what matter is, we must frankly answer that we do not know—that is, in a scientific sense. Matter is commonly supposed to be something which exerts force, but the latter term, as has often been pointed out, "is a *how* and not a *why*," "a description of *how* bodies change their motion." "So long then" (I am quoting) "as we consider the universe made up of things moving and altering each other's motion, we are on safe ground, . . . we may call the moving things matter, but we must ever bear in mind that the moving things may be the last things in the world which accord with the popular conception of matter, they may even be its negation. What if the ultimate atom upon which we build up the apparently substantial realities of the external world be an absolute vacuum? or what if matter be only non-matter in motion? . . . Descartes held extension, not impenetrability, the essence of matter. 'Give me extension and motion, and I will construct the world,' he cried."[1]

[1] Karl Pearson, "Matter and Soul," pp. 5–9. Published by the Sunday Lecture Society.

But some hypotheses have denied even extension to matter. Boscovitch assumed that its ultimate elements were mathematical points—that is, points without extension—endowed with attractive and repulsive forces. Thus matter would only be distinguished from non-matter by the fact of its motion.[1] Others suggest that the supposed atom of matter may be a void, the boundaries of which are endowed with a certain amount of energy; others, that it is a change in the shape of space, —an idea which it would take too long to explain, but one which implies the existence of space of more dimensions than three; while others — and this notion commends itself to many very thoughtful minds — regard matter as a particular phase of motion, a vortex ring in that impalpable something which appears to fill all space and which we call the ether.[1]

I do not profess to comprehend all these theories, and the last obviously still leaves open the question, What is the ether? but I have recounted them to

[1] Karl Pearson, "Matter and Soul," p. 9.   [2] Ibid., pp. 9-11.

show that physicists of the highest ability regard matter from a point of view very different from that of the older metaphysicians, and that there are those who would be prepared to consider it as something very like a mode of manifestation of energy. This, however, removes matter in its origin into the sphere of spirit, to use the ordinary distinction; we have hunted it down through the region of the knowable, believing its capture to be inevitable, and lo, it has slipped away from us into the region of the unknowable! The man of science and the Christian alike have to confess their ignorance of what the ground-stuff of the known universe really is, but the latter adds, "I believe it to be a mode of the manifestation of God."

We begin now dimly to understand why the work of creation is ascribed to the Word. "All things were made by Him."[1] Employing human terminology—and here we cannot be too careful in remembering its inadequacy—the word *manifesta-*

[1] St. John i. 3.

D

tion implies at least an antithesis; there must be one to perceive and one to be perceived. God, not revealing Himself, in relation to such a race as ours, is not God at all. I do not say that He may not be; but I mean this: Suppose you are thinking and do not express your thought—then, so far as the rest of the world goes, you might as well never have thought at all. True, the thought exists for yourself, and is not dependent upon *our* conscious-ness; but, as we can only be made conscious of it by its expression, the thought, for us, is non-existent. Thus, from our point of view, the abso-lute existence of God is one thing; the existence in relation to man is another. It is with the latter only that we have to deal; and in this sense it is a mere truism to assert that, for man, God only exists through man's consciousness of His existence, which consciousness I suppose, of course, to be set in action by Him.

Thus, as among ourselves speech or its equivalent is, or at least should be, the expression of thought, and so is the only mode by which we can impart of our own consciousness to our fellows, so the Logos, in its double sense of word and reason, is *the thought of God in its expression to us.* As, with ourselves, the uttered word cannot be recalled, as it may acquire, in a certain sense, a life apart from the speaker, and yet has a unity of nature with him, for it was a mode of self-manifestation,— so we can dimly understand why a personality is claimed for the Word; we can see the significance of the analogies, more or less imperfect, which have been so often stated by writers on the subject that it is needless for me to repeat them. But in applying to the region which is beyond our experiences and transcends our thoughts terms founded exclusively on these, we must ever remember that they are symbols only, and these most inadequate.

I have deemed it unnecessary to dwell upon an aspect of the subject which has been often discussed, the world as a manifestation of Order and Mind, because, although the teleological arguments which were once deemed satisfactory have had to be abandoned, all, or almost all, thinkers would admit

—however widely they differ in their terminology
and their theological opinions—that, in our sur-
roundings, we perceive the traces of a mighty plan,
as well as the working of an infinite energy. But
on this I do not enlarge, partly because it has so
often engaged attention, partly because it is a
question belonging rather to theism than to Christianity.

Are we then losers by the progress of science?
Its result during late years has been to extend the
reign of law, to indicate underlying unity in
apparent diversity, to replace imperfect anthropomorphic conceptions by ideas of a Creator which,
if more vaguely outlined, are grander far.

If then, Christian theology asserts that in the one
God a distinction, to which we apply the term
Personal, existed before all time; this difficulty
began in theism, and is metaphysical, not scientific.
But the existence of an *eternal* distinction becomes
less startling when science aids in demonstrating
the inseparability of our methods of thought from
the order in which we live. Time and extension

involve the idea of change, development, progress. Yet these may be relative; local, not universal: may be—to take a very imperfect illustration—as it is with us when Nature seems to be at rest and the stillness absolute, yet within the closed petals of a flower a colony of tiny insects is in full activity, and their little world resounds with a hum of life, inaudible to the most attentive ear. Moreover, when science in the region of the phenomenal begins to pass beyond the concrete, and mass is replaced by potency, which from the first seems an expression of purpose, it sounds less startling to say that the universe itself is a manifestation of the thought of God.

The old difficulty of course remains, which in my opinion stands where it did: Does God reveal Himself to man? This we cannot *prove*, yet, we can believe, because the indirect evidence is strong.[1] If this be so, then we can accept the statements as to the Divine Nature made by the Founder of

---

[1] This subject was discussed in the Boyle Lectures for 1890. See " Old Truths in Modern Lights."

Christianity. We do not profess to understand them, as we do inductions from our own observations, but we can perceive their meaning and be content to admit that in this way only ideas transcending our experience could be represented to us. So doing, we are assured by watching the marvels with which we are environed, that all is of God and from God, that He "fulfils Himself in many ways," and that if now and again He has spoken in tones which were strange, and through expressions which were unfamiliar, He is revealed to us, alike in the stillness of our secret thoughts and in the round of daily life, by means of the fair world which He has made, and in which He has placed us for a season, till it please Him to show us what the eye hath not seen nor the ear heard, for such things belong to the order, not of Time, but of Eternity.

LECTURE II.

THE HOLY SPIRIT.

"When the Comforter is come, Whom I will send unto you from the Father, even the Spirit of Truth, Which proceedeth from the Father . . . He shall guide you into all the truth."—ST. JOHN xv. 26; xvi. 13 (R. V.).

SPIRIT and Matter, whatever the terms may mean, generally connote ideas which are antithetical, if not antagonistic. On the second of these I have already made some remarks: the present occasion [1] invites me to touch, however diffidently, upon the first. That God is a Spirit is a principle of theism, not of Christianity only. Hence, in accordance with the limitation which I have imposed upon myself, I shall not discuss this preliminary question, though I may have to refer to it indirectly in dealing with the doctrine of the Christian Church in regard to the Holy Spirit.

[1] The lecture was given on Whitsunday.

This doctrine did not assume a special pro-
minence at so early an epoch as that of which I
spoke last Sunday. As the founder of Christianity
had claimed to be, in the fullest sense of the
phrase, Son of God, the nature of the Logos and the
significance of this claim speedily became, as was to
be expected, a field for speculation and a subject
of controversy. At that time the intellectual
position of the Palestine upland, the birthplace
of Christianity, corresponded with its geographical.
It parted two areas of thought as it parted the
waters of two seas. Christianity could not move
outwards without coming into relations, whether
hostile or friendly, with Oriental mysticism on the
one side, and with Greek philosophy on the other.
Each of these, apart from historical necessities,
tended to force to the front the controversies which
have for their centre such a declaration as this:
"The Word became flesh and dwelt among us."
But in regard to the Holy Spirit, the phrases of
Scripture were accepted, as a rule, without any
attempt at further precision of statement. This

is indicated, assuredly, though indirectly, by the fact that in the Creed of Nicæa the elaborate statements as to the Word Incarnate were followed by the single simple clause, "I believe in the Holy Ghost." But in a little more than half a century the necessity of precision on this point also became obvious, and the clauses were added which conclude the Creed as it stands in the Prayer-book, with the exception of one phrase. Subsequently, in the Western Church, the words ran thus: "I believe in the Holy Ghost, the Lord and Giver of life, Who proceedeth from the Father and the Son, Who with the Father and the Son together is worshipped and glorified. Who spake by the prophets." The Eastern Church objected to the addition of the words "and the Son" as unauthorized, and liable to be misunderstood, and the controversy at last became so sharp between them that, just after the middle of the eleventh century, they parted asunder.

On this, and other refined theological distinctions, I do not intend to dwell. They are the results of

E

deductive reasoning from the words of revelation
on the part of acute dialecticians, and thus are
not likely to be materially affected by progress in
thought which has been mainly due to inductive
processes.   I shall content myself with a few words
on the broader aspect of the doctrine enunciated
in the Creed of Constantinople.

It must not be forgotten that, while in the
English version and in theological literature, two
terms are employed to designate the Third Person
in the Triune Godhead, viz. the Holy Spirit and
the Holy Ghost,—the substantives are renderings of
one and the same word in the original Greek.
This word is πνεῦμα. In its everyday sense it
means breath, or a wind,—in short, air in motion :
it may admit the idea of intermittence, but hardly
that of violence. Then, it is occasionally used
figuratively to signify life, and so is applied in a
theological sense to express spirit—itself a similar
extension of the Latin word *spiritus*. *Pneuma*
does not, as a rule, signify *ghost*, in the popular
sense of that word. In the New Testament it is

used, not only for the spirit of God (whether in the minor sense as an influence, or the major one as God Himself), but also for antagonistic influences. It is used also for that element in the nature of man which distinguishes him from the mere animals, to which only body and life are ascribed.[1] In the discourse with Nicodemus the word is one which is rendered here by *wind*, there by *spirit*. We may, then, say that the word *pneuma* connotes movement, viewed apart from the thing moved, for the popular mind did not attribute materiality to the air. It connotes life apart from its physical basis, and influence, to use a wide term, apart from its subject. In the theological sense life and influence are the dominant ideas. In the Nicene Creed we speak of the Holy Ghost as Giver of Life.

But what is life? We have made long strides in biology during the present century, but we do not seem to be much more able to answer this question.

[1] See "The Threefold Nature of Man," in "Old Truths in Modern Lights," p. 114.

Scientific men of one school affirm their belief that, whatever life be, it differs essentially from the forces called physical. To their minds the beginning of life, no less than the beginning of matter, requires an exercise of creative power. Others place life in the same category as the physical forces, like electricity, light, heat; to them it is a form of the manifestation of energy. They discern in matter itself "the promise and potency of all terrestrial life."[1] They refuse to draw any hard and fast line between man himself and the dust from which he is said to have been fashioned, though they confess that they know of no synthetic process by which life can be produced, no method whereby the known forms of energy can be transformed into it. Still it is obviously admitted by either school that life is a mystery— the one affirming it to be inscrutable, the other frankly allowing that its solution, if within the sphere of hope, seems very far from attainment.

[1] Tyndall, Belfast Address to British Association, "Fragments of Science," p. 524.

But whatever life may be, it is inseparable from and underlain by the idea of motion. To this we seem ultimately brought in all modern philosophical speculation. As an example, I will quote some sentences from an author whose bias certainly is anything but favourable to Christianity or even to theism.[1] He writes thus: "It is no dogma, but downright common sense to assert that if everything in the universe were brought to rest, the universe would cease to be perceptible, or for all human purposes it would cease to be. The sensible existence of matter is entirely dependent on the existence of motion." Indeed, this matter itself, as I indicated in my last lecture, is considered by not a few as localized energy. But if it be asked what is energy, we can only reply "the power of doing work." This obviously is an explanatory periphrasis, but it is not an answer. It asserts a certain reality of existence to the universe, as against an extreme idealism, but at the same time it is forced to take refuge in what can hardly

[1] Karl Pearson, "Matter and Soul," p. 6.

be distinguished from a metaphysical concept. But on this aspect of the question I will not dwell; I desire only to insist upon this, that in the field of science, the whole sensible universe, including life and its phenomena, is at last found to be included in this definition, " energy in action."

It may, however, be asked whether, in making this statement, we have not overlooked consciousness, than which nothing is more certain. But in the field of pure science what line can be drawn between consciousness and life, or, for the matter of hat, between that which lives and that which does not live? We can of course distinguish them as objects of thought, as, for instance, we can mentally separate electricity and light, or a cannon-ball and the heat generated by its impact, but we come at last to different modes of an underlying something.

I do not, for my present purpose, dispute the possibility that life may be either a special and unique mode of the manifestation of energy or a special synthesis of certain modes of energy—indeed, this is my own opinion;—all I wish to emphasize is that, in so far as science can deal with it, life cannot be removed from the category of the physical. Its differences, if such there be, cannot be demonstrated by science. This must be agnostic in such questions as the origin of matter, the beginning of life, the existence of soul.

Do not, however, misunderstand me. It does not follow that because we cannot *prove* a thing to exist, we are precluded from believing in it. Indirect evidence may be strong, though the direct evidence may be weak. As we do not become pure idealists because we cannot accurately define or comprehend either matter or life, so we do not declare that the immortality of the soul is impossible because we do not know of anything which does not die.

That a spiritual world is a reality, is a fact in the order of the universe no less than the material; this, if you like so to call it, is a theological dogma (or, as I should prefer to put it, a deduction from certain statements which we think to be true, *i.e.* from a revelation). As I have already said, we are driven back to our original assumption—the possibility and probability of a revelation; but we have found in the process of discussion that all this material universe, that every phenomenon of which we can take cognizance, that the physical basis of this conscious "ego," proves to be only some mode or form of energy in action. Without this energy (be it what it may) there is no volition, no consciousness, no life, no matter—nothingness.

Does this seem a mere outbreak of theological mysticism? Well, it is only stating in another form the conclusions of philosophies, which at the present day are in high favour with many. Schopenhauer maintains that beyond matter, behind force, constituting all existence, is *will*—not, indeed, the will of a Personality, but a mere blind impulse to live. Von Hartmann adopts the same view, but adds as a metaphysical principle of equal value, that of unconscious thought in the All. So potent is this will-force, that the redemption suggested by each, the panacea for the miseries of life, is "ceasing to will;" then, in Von Hartmann's scheme, which is the more comprehensive of the two, "Consciousness will suffice to hurl back the total actual volition into nothingness, by which the process and the world ceases . . . without leaving any residuum whatever, whereby the process might be continued." "This," as it has been truly remarked, "is salvation with a vengeance. The universe is saved from misery by being reduced to nothing." [1]

From the creative let me turn to another aspect of this omnipotent energy. We learn that the conservation of energy is an established and fundamental principle in physics. It "asserts that no portion of energy can be put out of existence, and no amount of energy can be brought into existence by any process at our command." [2] Is not this tantamount to admitting that energy belongs to the category of the things unknowable in themselves, though cognizable in their effects ; or that, in theological language, it is a manifestation

[1] Bishop Moorhouse, "Dangers of the Apostolic Age," p. 67.
[2] P. G. Tait, "Recent Advances in Physical Science," p. 17.

F

of the Divinity ? In matter we see, in one aspect, thought in expression; in another, energy in action; the one and the other centring in and proceeding forth from the unknown God.

This, an objector may say, sounds very much like pantheism. Undoubtedly it does. There is a true side to pantheism which has often been forgotten by overhasty Christians. The distinction between the statements, God is everything, and Everything is a manifestation of God, exists rather in the classification of thought than in actuality. But I have not enunciated the converse statement that, in the usual sense of the word, everything is God. On this, the great difficulty of human thought, the enigma older than Christianity, we find, I think, that some light is indirectly thrown by another statement of physicists concerning energy.

They tell us that the quantity of energy cannot be changed, for it remains the same, however great the number of transformations. "But it has another and even more curious property : . . . .

change is essential to the existence of phenomena such as we observe; and that this change may take place, it is necessary that there should be constant transformation of energy. But some forms of energy are more capable of being transformed than others; and every time that a transformation takes place there is always a tendency to pass, at least in part, from a higher or more easily transformable, to a lower or less easily transformable form."[1]

Thus the universe, as it waxes old, is dying, slowly dying. "In the far distant future . . . the quantities of matter and energy will remain absolutely as they now are—the matter unchanged alike in quantity and quality, but collected together under the influence of its mutual gravitation, so that there remains no potential energy of detached portions of matter: the energy also unchanged in quantity, but entirely transformed in quality to the low form of heat so diffused as to produce uniformity of temperature."[2]

[1] P. G. Tait, "Recent Advances in Physical Science," p. 20.
[2] Ibid. p. 21.

This second great physical principle—of the Dissipation of Energy—limits the apparently pantheistic conclusions to which we might otherwise be led. Suppose we regard matter as a localization of Divine power, as "man's limitation of God's Infinity," to use a bold similitude. We are at any rate forced to admit that, in whatever sense we apply the term, it is a manifestation of God. But in the act of manifestation it incurs a liability to the law of death; each transformation lowers it, if the phrase be permitted, in the scale of things created; the effective power, the capacity for adaptation is gradually lost, till at last it may have deviated so far from its original likeness, that to our limited vision it may seem to be arrayed against the source from which it proceeded.

In the fantastic dreams of æons and emanations common to many Gnostic sects, there was a germ of true philosophy, for these tended to bridge that seemingly impassable gulf between the conditioned and the unconditioned. In the descent of the ladder of existence no upward step is possible without the

help of an external power, for in every retrans-
formation from the lower to the higher forms some
energy appears to be lost. This, no doubt, is not
really the case. The energy is still in existence, but
is no longer available for our purposes. Thus, for
all progress, for all evolution, a price has to be
paid. Speaking figuratively, the universe is like
a man who is living upon his capital, and this
process must end in destitution. This, then, is the
alternative which confronts us: God must be our
deliverer, or the end inevitably is nothingness.

Which of these are we to accept? We do not
hesitate what answer to return. We believe in a
revelation. From it we learn that through the
Divine thought the universe became. "Through
the Word He made the æons," says the author of
the Epistle to the Hebrews; that—the making
manifest, the objective side of revelation, if we may
so call it—is the function of the Son, of the Second
Person in the Trinity. But the work of quickening, of vivifying, of infusing a new energy or
counteracting the natural tendency to dissipation—

pardon the inadequacy of the term—*that* is the work of the Holy Spirit, called emphatically "the Giver of Life."

This is in full accord with the words of Scripture. It is the Holy Spirit Who is said to work in prophets and teachers, to guide, to influence, to quicken the soul of every child of God. At each new departure in the early history of Christendom his Name appears. In the mystery of the Incarnation; in the consecration, if the phrase be permissible, of the Word made Flesh to the work of Redemption at the waters of Jordan; in the first ordination of the faithful disciples, when that work had been virtually completed by the Resurrection; in that greater ordination of the complete twelve, when it had actually been ended by the Ascension; in the command to Peter to open the door of the fold; in the mission of Paul and Barnabas to the world;—in each and all of these the agency of the Holy Ghost is asserted. He spake—so saith the Scripture—by the mouths of prophets, psalmists, and teachers in the days of old, in the brightening

twilight of the dawn, before the sun of righteousness arose. He spake again by the mouths of
apostles and preachers, of martyrs and saints—
men and women "full of the Holy Ghost." Shall
we say that His work is ended? Nay, His voice
is yet heard in the thoughts that glow and in the
words that burn, in every call to men to rise "on
stepping-stones of their dead selves to higher
things." All that strengthens us to suffer, all that
nerves us to resist evil, all that encourages us to
hope—all is the work of Him Who can quicken this
frail human body with the life which is eternal!

May we apply to the Holy Spirit the term
"Person"? Certainly, if we exclude those ideas
of limitation which arise from its common uses
among ourselves,—if we regard it as a symbol to
express a fact of thought. But on this I hope to
say something more in my next lecture. Here it
will be enough to repeat that we accept the distinction in the Unity of the Trinity, not as a
discovery of reason, but as a revelation. It has
been my endeavour to indicate that even in the

order of which our senses can take cognizance, we can discern analogies, which render these mysteries less startling, I dare not say more comprehensible. In the Logos, we see the Divine Thought in expression, the Wisdom manifested, the realization— to use a Platonic phrase—of the Archetypal ideas. In the Holy Spirit we contemplate the Divine Energy in action, the Lord and Giver of life, by Whom, by Whose quickening influence man can live not only physically, can know that there are spiritual realities behind and beyond the things of sense, and can venture to declare that his own personality may be delivered from the common law of death, and is not doomed to attain at last, as its only possible goal, to the Nirwana of dissipated energy, to the loss of individual consciousness by absorption in the Soul of the Universe, to an eternal silence and an eternal inactivity.

LECTURE III.

THE HOLY TRINITY.

"Make disciples of all the nations, baptizing them into the Name of the Father and of the Son and of the Holy Ghost."— ST. MATT. xxviii. 19 (R.V.).

"CHRISTIANITY inherited from Judaism, together with the Scriptures of the Old Testament, their fundamental principle of the unity of God;"[1] but is distinguished from all other creeds by the doctrine of the Trinity. In saying this, I do not forget that there are triads in other theologies, as in Neoplatonism and Ophite-gnosticism, in Buddhism and Hinduism; but the resemblance of these to the Trinity of the Church Catholic is little more than superficial, however important it may be as a stage in the education of our race and

[1] H. M. Gwatkin, "Studies of Arianism," p. 6.

G

a preparation for the fuller light. The doctrine passes human understanding, it transcends human powers of thought; it is by revelation, not by discovery. It has, indeed, afforded scope for the most profound reflection, the utmost precision of philosophic statement; it may be called a triumph of theology, to have steered between a mono-theism which would have deprived the Incarnation of its full significance, and a tritheism which would have been only a limitation of the ancient polytheism, and would have led back to the same results: but for the ground of that theology, of all that system of deductive argument, we must fall back upon, "It is written." ? ? ? ? ?

A Trinity in Unity at first sight seems, to a mind which is scientific rather than metaphysical in its bias, to be a contradiction in terms, the assertion of an impossibility. Here, if anywhere, we might exclaim, "Credo quia incredibile." This, in a sense, is so; but it will be my endeavour, I trust with all reverence, to inquire whether we cannot find, in the order of which our senses can take cognizance, some analogies which may render the doctrinal statements of the Church Catholic less startling to the scientific thinker.

It may be well to commence by a brief statement of the doctrine, because its difficulty naturally has a deterrent effect upon our minds, and renders us readily contented with a very vague conception as to what it really means. The doctrine is nowhere more clearly or precisely enunciated than in the creed which bears, though erroneously, the name of Athanasius. In this respect we must admit that ancient confession of the Western Church to have a high value, whatever may be our views as to the propriety of using it in public worship, or as to the validity of one or two adventitious expressions of opinion therein.[1]

These, then, are its statements as to the "Catholic Faith:" "We worship one God in Trinity, and Trinity in Unity; neither confounding the Persons, nor dividing the Substance. For

[1] I refer, of course, to the so-called "damnatory clauses."

there is one Person of the Father, another of the
Son, and another of the Holy Ghost. But the
Godhead of the Father, of the Son, and of the Holy
Ghost is all one." A number of explanatory
clauses follow, in the course of which it is said,
"As we are compelled by the Christian verity to
acknowledge every Person by Himself to be God
and Lord: so are we forbidden by the Catholic
Religion to say, There be three Gods, or three
Lords." The whole' concludes thus: "In this
Trinity none is afore or after other; none is
greater or less than another; but the whole three
Persons are co-eternal together and co-equal. So
that in all things, as is aforesaid, the Unity in
Trinity and the Trinity in Unity is to be
worshipped."

It is obvious that the meaning of this elaborate
doctrinal summary is inseparably dependent on that
of two terms which are employed therein. These
are "Person" and "Substance."[1] "Neither con-

[1] See Hatch, "Influence of Greek Ideas," ch. ix.; Smith and
Wace, "Dictionary of Christian Biography, etc.," s.v. "Trinity;"
and Gwatkin, "Studies of Arianism," chs. i.–iii.

founding the Persons nor dividing the Substance."
" Person " is the rendering of the Latin word
Persona. This meant primarily a "mask" or "false
head " worn by actors, whence it might be employed
in a figurative sense. Thence it was extended to
designate the character sustained, whether on the
stage of the theatre or of the world ; and from
this to the actor himself, when it was sometimes
restricted like the English word " personage."
Also, especially in a legal sense, it signified
" persons " as opposed to " things " and " actions."
The other word translates the Latin *Substantia*,
which indicates that of which a thing consists, as a
subject of thought, rather than as an object of sense,
though the distinction cannot always be strictly
maintained. But, as speculative theology in the
Christian Church was more of Eastern than of
Western origin, we must go back to the terms in
the Greek language which the Latin words were
intended to represent. In that long period of
subtle speculation and stormy discussion which
began even before the second century and was

hardly closed at the end of the fifth, more than two terms were employed in controversial theology, and a greater precision of statement was attainable owing to the distinction already drawn by Greek philosophy between the φαινόμενα, the objective or physical aspect of things, and the νοούμενα, or mental concepts of the same, which are not accessible to the senses. Terms expressive of the latter are, to the scientific man, symbols; to the metaphysician, realities. The terminology of Christian controversy was borrowed from Greek philosophy, so that the above-named distinction must be carefully borne in mind. In the disputes on the subject of the Trinity, at any rate during the period with which we are more particularly concerned, three terms appeared in the fore-front of the battle. These were *Ousia* (Οὐσία), *Hypostasis* ('Υπόστασις), and *Prosōpon* (Πρόσωπον). The last had nearly the same sense as the Latin *Persona*, but did not connote so emphatically an individual separate existence. Hence it was even employed by the anti-Trinitarian Sabellius to express the

three temporal aspects, the existence of which he
was willing to admit in the One God. Of the
other terms, *Ousia* (Οὐσία) had been used in
philosophic diction in three distinct senses : namely,
as the material—the ground-stuff of things, equivalent to *hylé* (ὕλη); as a sensible material thing
which in a predication must always be a subject ;
and as the common element in the classes into
which sensible material things may be grouped—
the "form or ideal essence." [1] In process of time
the meaning of the term, owing to diversity of use,
became yet more uncertain, but in the Platonic terminology, which represented one of the two great
schools of thought, *Ousia* designated the "idea" or
"form," the inherence of which makes any object
that which it actually is—its essence or being. [2] In
Stoic terminology a noetic conception practically
identical was expressed by *Hypostasis*. But in
the course of later controversy a distinction between
the two terms was drawn, and generally accepted ;

---

[1] Hatch, "Influence of Greek Ideas," p. 278.
[2] "Dictionary of Christian Biography," s.v. "Trinity."

and *Ousia* was defined as a "universal," denoting
that which was the common element in a group, as
in the various species of a genus, the different
individuals of a species, and the like; while *Hypostasis* expressed that which made the individual
what he is, "which in fact constitutes individual
existence." Thus Catholic theologians, in rejecting
both "the Arian Trinity of one increate and
two created beings, and the Sabellian Trinity of
temporal aspects (Πρόσωπα) of the One," acknow-
ledged, "not three individuals, but three eternal
aspects ('Υποστάσεις) of the Divine, facing inward
on each other as well as outward on the world."[1]
Thus the word Person in the so-called Athanasian
Creed must not be fettered overmuch by its popular
use, but expresses the *Hypostasis* of Greek theologians, and the clauses therein must be regarded
as an expansion of the statement of Athanasius
himself, that in the Godhead there were three
Hypostases in one *Ousia*. The distinction obviously is noetic; it does not belong to the

---

[1] H. M. Gwatkin, "Studies of Arianism," p. 9.

Phenomena (Φαινόμενα) of which science, strictly speaking, can take cognizance, for it cannot be tested by the evidence of the senses or by inductions directly founded thereon. But is it so absolutely contradictory to the analogies of the order of the sensible universe that we may dismiss it as a chimæra of a metaphysical cloud-land?

Consider the world of living creatures. Here, at first sight, distinct individuality seems a necessary idea. But not seldom in plants this individuality is, so to say, separable. Not a few of them can be divided into parts, which will then become separate individuals, incapable of subsequent fusion into one. The value of this analogy may, however, be disputed by refusing to admit that consciousness can be attributed to plant-life. Turn, then, to the animal world, wherein the existence of some form of consciousness can hardly be denied. In certain of the lowest organisms, as we call them, there is the same separability. In what does the individuality of some of the Protozoa consist? Nay, here, I believe, coalition after separation may occasionally

H

take place. But also in those of somewhat higher grade we find a diversity co-existent with a unity. Such is the case with some of the compound forms, as they are called, among the Cœlenterates. A Hydrozoan, for instance, such as the sea-fir (*Sertularia*), consists of a number of polypites connected by a common tissue, the one being related to the other, to use a rough simile, as buds just bursting from the bark of a twig are to the woody axis. The life of the whole colony is a common one, yet it is individualized in each polypite, though we may express doubts whether even these can be always regarded as complete individuals; for the reproductive process does not invariably take place in them, but may result from an independent action, the formation of a new and separate group of structures at some part of the common but less highly differentiated stem.

Again, to take another group in the same subkingdom—the corals. Here, also, a similar common unspecialized tissue uniting the specialized parts is often found. How, in such case, are we to form a perfect mental concept of the individual? We cannot wholly separate the more specialized from the less specialized tissues, nor any two of the latter one from another. With these creatures also, among the possible modes of multiplication, is the following:—A single polypite gradually separates into two or more, which ultimately become perfectly complete in themselves. Follow in thought the gradual change from one individual life to two individual lives, and see whether the continuity of existence does not bring you to something very like two aspects of a common essence " facing inward upon themselves as well as outward upon the world." I might carry on the same line of illustration to the embryonic stages of creatures much higher in organization, but, as there are obvious difficulties in entering upon the discussion of some of the details, a suggestion of it may suffice.

It may be urged as an objection that I have found my analogies among the lowest organisms or lowest stages of an organism. That is true, but we must not forget that the distinctive characteristics of all living creatures are determined, how we know not, at a very early stage in their existence. At a time when it would be impossible for us, owing to the absence of characteristics, to predict the position to which the embryo will attain in the animal kingdom, this already is irrevocably decided; the future organization is potentially present, is hypostatically distinguished. We must also remember that in the present order the ultimate result of high organization is death. Not only is the highly organized animal more easily killed, but also the race is more speedily destroyed by changes in its environment. The very specialization of function which is the cause of its temporary prosperity, is also, inasmuch as the world's order is not eternal, the cause of its ultimate destruction, since, in the process of differentiation, it has become less capable of further change. Pessimistic as the statement may seem, it is true, in a certain sense of the words, that self-improvement is only another name for self-destruction.

But development and specialization belong to the temporal order; they have no place in that which is eternal. The thing with its potentialities, the thing with these accomplished, may be one in the sight of Him, in Whose order time and space may have an existence which is equally objective and equally subjective. If, to express our meaning, we fall back for a moment on a Platonic phrase, we may say that the pretemporal Form in the Divine Mind admits of no comparative terms, and that in the progress from the monad to man, just as in the progress from the embryo to the adult, we may only be witnessing its evolution in the order of the temporal and the phenomenal. Organization, specialization, may be only the focusing, as it were, of the archetypal idea on the screen of the material; the image grows distinct before our eyes, yet it might be said to exist in reality, though it was not perceptible by our senses, at every stage of the process.

But I admit, as I said, that the analogy is imperfect. I bring it forward only to indicate that, in the order cognizable by scientific methods, a personal existence is not so simple a question as at first sight it might appear. However, seeing that we are involved in difficulties whenever we try to follow up the great mystery of life, let us turn for a moment to the inorganic world, from which this disturbing factor is eliminated. One might reasonably expect that substances chemically identical would correspond in their attributes, but this is by no means always the case: they may differ so widely that their identity would be unsuspected by any person who was debarred from using those particular tests which establish that identity. These differences, also, in many cases are conspicuous, and are persistent. They are, in short, among inorganic bodies the equivalent of a personality among living creatures. The physical properties—such as hardness, action upon light, heat, electricity—the geometrical relations of the outward forms, and the internal structures may be all different: they may be as strongly contrasted as in the well-known case of

graphite and the diamond,[1] and yet they are
chemically identical, the atoms are the same;
the bricks, so to say, of which the structure is
built, are the same; but some difference in the
method of putting them together, some difference
in the environment, as we say, cloaking our
ignorance by a phrase, or some difference in the
architect's plan, as we might affirm, not less
reasonably, has resulted in this marked and
persistent diversity. Of this allotropy, as it is
called by chemists, there are some cases where
there is no distinction of outward form or of ordinary physical properties, yet the relations to other
materials are altered, as in the case of ozone and
oxygen.

I mention these cases as illustrations only. I do
not presume to measure the unconditioned by the
conditioned; but if I were to adopt the terminology of the metaphysician, and say that rutile,

---

[1] Graphite (the material of "black-lead" pencils) is among the
softest of minerals, diamond is the hardest; the one is opaque, the
other transparent; they differ also in their crystalline forms, and
in other respects: yet each is crystallized carbon.

brookite, and anatase [1] (three forms of titanic oxide), or graphite, cliftonite,[2] and diamond (three forms of carbon), were three *hypostases* in one *ousia*, it would be difficult to charge me with a misuse of language.

But, in addition to this, the whole tendency of modern thought has been to emphasize the underlying unity of Nature, and to refer its differences to a difference of position rather than to a difference of essence. The older views concerning matter, namely, that the universe could be reduced to groups of ultimate atoms, each essentially different from the other, influenced the mind in the opposite direction; it favoured the idea of initial diversity, independence, and multiplicity: but the modern hypotheses concerning matter, which I mentioned in a former lecture,[3] have had the

[1] Not to mention other differences, these are crystallized in accordance with different laws.

[2] Cliftonite is a very rare form of carbon, in some respects resembling graphite, but it is much harder, and takes the crystalline form of the diamond. It has been found in meteorites (Fletcher, *Mineralogical Magazine*, vol. vii. p. 121).

[3] See pp. 14–17.

opposite tendency. Suppose, for instance, that Thomson is right, and that all matter consists of vortex rings in an imponderable, impalpable " something ; " then all its diversities, all its various properties, must consist, in their later stages, in differences of synthesis, but at an earlier one in differences of relative position. In this case, also, the unity of *ousia*, or substance, the diversity of *hypostases* might be affirmed.

In short, the distinctions with which our senses can deal must be ultimately explained by differences of position—that is, of mutual relationship. As we trace back, step by step, the history of matter, whether by experiment or in thought, the complex is simplified, the compounds are dissolved, the distinctive attributes disappear, pleomorphism [1] proves to be only a disguised unity. Still, as the pleomorphic representatives of this unity are so constant, so persistent, in the phenomenal world,

[1] The term employed in mineralogy to indicate the occurrence of any one substance in diverse " forms," as in the cases mentioned on pp. 55, 56.

I

the metaphysicians could fairly assert for each the existence of a noetic substratum; otherwise they might be reduced to the admission that there was only a single noetic concept in the universe.

These concepts, then, in position, must be not only relative to us, but also mutually relative to themselves. That is, the varied *hypostases* in the one *ousia* not only face outward on the world, but also inward on themselves.

I do not presume to say that this is an adequate explanation of the doctrine of the Holy Trinity. We may do well to remember the vision of Augustine of Hippo. As he wandered along the shore of the Tuscan Maremma,[1] wrapped in meditation, and vainly seeking to solve this mystery, he thought that he saw a child who was engaged in filling a small vessel from the sea, and emptying the water into a hole in the sand. He asked the child what he was about. The little one answered

---

[1] At Torre de Bertaldo, by the mouth of the Minio. See Hare, "Days near Rome," vol. ii. p. 317; Jameson, "Sacred and Legendary Art," vol. i. p. 297.

that he was emptying the sea. "That is impossible!" exclaimed Augustine. "Not more impossible," replied the child, "than it is for thee to
explain the mystery on which thou art now meditating." So it must be with us : the mystery of
the Divine relationships, of the Godhead itself,
cannot be grasped by our finite powers. Granted
the possibility of a revelation, if only we are satisfied that we have this in the person of Christ,
the doctrine of the Trinity can be established
deductively from the words of Scripture as it was
by the theologians of the primitive Church. It
receives an immense, though an indirect, support
from the fact that all other hypotheses can be
shown by logical necessity to lead us back to a
fruitless monotheism, to an immoral pantheism, or
to a degrading polytheism. It satisfies the deeper
cravings of humanity. To quote the words of one
too early lost to the Church of our own day :[1]
" While philosophy with increasing hopelessness

---

[1] Aubrey Moore, author of the singularly able essay on "The
Christian Doctrine of God," contributed to "Lux Mundi."

was asking, 'How can we have a real unity which shall be not a barren and dead unity, but shall include differences?' Christianity, with its doctrine of God, was arguing that that which was an unsolved contradiction for non-Christian thought, was a necessary corollary of the Christian Faith." We may add, I trust, that the progress of inductive investigation and deductive reasoning, instead of making the doctrine of the Trinity in Unity more startling and paradoxical, has lightened its difficulty by showing that in the order of nature there is a unity in its differences, and there may be relative differences in its unity.

LECTURE IV.

THE INCARNATION.

"The Word became flesh, and dwelt among us."—St. John i. 14 (R.V.).

THE Incarnation of the Word—God manifest in man and as man, is the central mystery of Christianity. It can be contemplated from more than one point of view. Assuming, for a moment, that such an event is not antecedently incredible, it may be considered in regard either to its significance and place in the order of the world, or to its purpose, if the term be permitted; that is, to use the technical phrases, in its Christological or its Soteriological aspect. At present I restrict myself, as far as possible, to the former.

A belief in an incarnation, in some sense of the word, is not peculiar to Christianity. Polytheism

was thoroughly anthropomorphic in its conceptions, and invested its gods with the form, the appetites, and even the passions of men. This, however, may perhaps be termed a personification, rather than an incarnation; for it was not supposed that the bodies of the gods were identical with those of men. And even when the former were asserted to have assumed a true human body, this incarnation would be termed, in the language of theology, docetic rather than real.

A nearer parallel is found in Hinduism, with its *avatars*. It has often been pointed out, especially by opponents of Christianity, that in Krishna, the eighth *avatar* of Vishnu, there are many points of correspondence with the history recorded in the Gospels. This, to those who believe that a unity of plan and purpose pervades all the diversity of this world's order, presents no special difficulty; for it may be said that the history of man's development is like unto a tree, which has not only its branches in the future, but also its roots in the past. But, in this particular case, there is good reason for doubting whether the instances of closer resemblance are not comparatively late accretions to the legend, which, instead of having an independent origin, have been really derived from Christianity. The latter certainly cannot have borrowed from Hinduism, for it is organically connected with Judaism. Two thousand years since the Hebrew world was expecting—at the present day it still expects—a Messias. He was to be, he is to be, more than man,—one, who, if not quite all that Christian theology affirms, should be, to quote the words of a weighty authority,[1] "far above the conditions of the most exalted of God's servants, even His angels: in short, so closely bordering on the Divine, that it was almost impossible to distinguish him therefrom."

The doctrine of the Catholic Church on the subject of the Incarnation cannot be more clearly stated than in the words of the so-called Athanasian Creed: "We believe and confess that our Lord

[1] Edersheim, "Life and Times of Jesus," bk. ii. ch. v. (vol. i. p. 179).

Jesus Christ, the Son of God, is God and Man; . . .
Perfect God, and perfect Man of a reasonable soul
and human flesh subsisting; Equal to the Father as
touching His Godhead, and inferior to the Father
as touching His Manhood. Who although He be
God and Man, yet He is not two, but one Christ;
One; not by conversion of the Godhead into flesh,
but by taking of the Manhood into God: One
altogether; not by confusion of Substance, but by
unity of Person." Almost every phrase in this
summary is a symbol of past controversy, a monu-
ment of a theological victory. It gives in systematic form the result of a deductive study of the
words of Scripture: needless to say, it expresses a
mystery deeper than the human mind can hope to
fathom.

It is not my intention to trace the history or
insist upon the importance of the above clauses.
Either would lie outside my present purpose.
Accepting them as an explanation of what is
meant by the Incarnation, let us ask whether
the great central mystery is so completely dis-

cordant with our environment that, in accepting
it, we are compelled to silence the protests of reason
by the assurances of faith? It does not so seem to
me, on the supposition that the ordinary views as
to the genesis of life and soul are in the main
correct. It is generally held that, whatever life
may be, it is not a simple attribute of matter, is
not to be classed with heat, electricity, magnetism;
that between ordinary matter and living matter
there is a great gulf fixed. It is also held that
between animals and men, or at least some men,
there is another such gulf:[1] that the death of the
body puts an end to the one, but not to the other;
the latter possessing, in addition to a perfect animal
organization, a spirit which is of God. If, then, we
believe that man has become a " living soul "—and
in this belief, remember, Christians do not stand
alone—then, unless we claim immortality for all
animals, we must admit that in one person the
nature of an immortal being and that of a mortal

[1] See "The Threefold Nature of Man" in "Old Truths in
Modern Lights," p. 114.

K

being are inseparably united. Here, then, the
higher has not been converted into the lower, but
the lower has been taken up into the higher. To
myself, at any rate, it appears that we cannot so
much as use the term volition without being confronted with this dilemma, that we must either
regard it as the result of a synthesis of organic
elements, and so cease to claim for it freedom, or
in asserting the latter, admit the existence of something which cannot be brought under any known
laws—that is, we must trespass on the domain of
the miraculous, though we shrink from using the
term.

Some perhaps might say: "We do not take offence
at the assertion of an Incarnation, for, whether you
would call us Pantheists or not, we certainly are
not advocates of a dualism which places the Divine
and the material in antagonism. We admit that it
is possible, inexplicable as it may be, that such a
union might take place, but we are unable to
believe in the birth from a virgin mother, because
it would be contrary to the order of nature."

Let me, then, touch briefly on this subject, difficult though it be to discuss. I may remark, at the outset, that if the birth of Jesus had been the result of the ordinary synthesis, then, in accordance with the order of nature, He would have been only a man. If, then, you are not prepared to admit this, if you are not content to reverence Christ merely as the most perfect man, you must fall back upon a miracle at some stage of His existence, for the union of the Godhead with the manhood is no part of the order of nature, so far as that is known.

Attempts have been made to elude the difficulty which is presented by the doctrine of the Incarnation by supposing that the Divine Nature united itself at some particular stage to that of a man, born in ordinary course; but to what does this modification amount? that we are willing to believe the assertion of a thing which lies wholly outside our experience, but not one which in any way seems to be contrary to our experience. I will not, indeed, go so far as to say that this distinction is entirely without value, but at any rate I am justified in pointing out that it does not enable us to get rid of miracle, but only to transfer its plane of operation.

Birth, we know, requires at a very early stage, in most living creatures, a synthesis of two elements, both extremely minute and apparently almost structureless.[1] The function of the one is mainly initiatory, though it also produces a permanent impression which results in the transmission of hereditary tendencies; the other develops into the future being. In this great marvel, much as we know of the "how," we are very ignorant of the "why." The union of two tiny rudimentary cells has for its result a being which presents, physically and mentally, strong resemblances to both parents! If I may venture to speak in the language of man concerning the Incarnation, the miracle consisted in this:—that the process of development began in one cell without the inter-

---

[1] The *ovum* of the most highly organized member of the animal kingdom is rather less than one hundredth of an inch in diameter (Huxley, "Man's Place in Nature," p. 65).

vention of the other: that, really, is all which we are asked to believe. A miracle undoubtedly, for that which otherwise would have remained incomplete was quickened to a perfect life. It was an exercise of Creative Force, an overshadowing of the Power of the Highest. This I am told, in words which, if not true, are mere rhapsody which borders on profanity. But at such an epoch in the history of mankind as the Advent of Christ on earth, might not a departure from the ordinary course be anticipated? If we are forced to admit miracle in the order of physical life, what wonder if it be required also in the order of the spiritual?

But, although it is quite true that, as a rule, the origin of an individual life is a synthetic process —not, however, of lifeless, but of living matter—we must nevertheless remember that the law is not universal. Cut off a slip from a plant, and it becomes a new individual, capable of bearing seed and propagating its kind in the usual way. Perhaps, however, you will demur to the value of this illustration, as being taken from the world of plants, not of animals. But in the latter, also, multiplication can take place in much the same way. Some animals divide themselves again and again; one individual becomes a host, by subdivision, not by generation in the ordinary sense.[1] We must also remember that in not a few living creatures no sexual distinctions are perceptible, in others the individual is bisexual. I do not forget the remarkable instances of what is called Parthenogenesis; for this at first sight might seem an exact parallel to the marvel which we are considering: but I do not press it, because I know that in some cases (though I am doubtful whether in all) the resemblance might be explained away. But I refer to the others to indicate—and thus far, at any rate, I have a right to use them—that the law of birth as a result of synthesis is not so universal and invariable as is commonly supposed.

It may be said that these apparent exceptions occur only among the lowest types of living creatures.

[1] W. H. Dallinger, "The Creator, and what we may know of the Method of Creation," p. 30.

It is true that they disappear, before the vertebrates are reached; but it must be remembered that even the most highly organized form of the latter, at one stage of its existence, although its future development in some mysterious way is already determined and may be regarded as potentially present, is itself actually indistinguishable from a protozoon. But it was at this very stage that the miracle which most startles our mind must have occurred. Are we not, in believing that a miracle was needed to produce from inert dead matter living protoplasm, with all its potentialities, and in hesitating to admit a similar miracle in one particular case, straining at a scientific gnat and swallowing a scientific camel? As it has been well said, "The mystery of life is as great and as deep in a monad as in a man."[1]

But, if we look further, and consider what the Incarnation means, we begin to understand why it behoved that Christ should not be born after the flesh. I will not now raise the soteriological question further than to say that One was needed

---

[1] W. H. Dallinger, "The Creator," p. 36.

who should be without sin. But the theological doctrine of original sin, regarded apart from some adventitious colouring, only states in another form the scientific doctrine of heredity. No child of human parents can be sinless; the animal nature is present from the first, and resists the impulses to conformity with external requirements; the development of the body outruns that of the mind, and for a considerable time the moral nature fights at a disadvantage with the physical. The fall of man, the innate infection of his nature, is a fact, an unquestionable awful fact in the world's order, even if every word in the third chapter of Genesis be allegorical. So that no one born after the flesh can be sinless. Perhaps, also, we should not leave out of sight the fact that to the human race everything connected with this synthesis is a fruitful source of evil. One, however, born as Christ is asserted to have been born, would be perfect man; for after the first beginning He would have passed through every stage of development and nutrition which belongs to a member of the human race. If the

Saviour of the world were to be man, He must be born, in a sense, in due course; but, to be sinless, He must be born out of due course. The course, of which we are told in revelation, is the most simple, the only conceivable one—to speak as a man—in which the perfection of the human nature, in union with the Divine nature, could have been secured.

Call us credulous believers in a miracle, if you will—that is, in an event which is inexplicable by any result of our experience; nay, which is contrary to, or, I should rather say, different from our experience. Be it so, but your scientific biologist, when he formulates his researches in the maxim, All that lives has a living parent,—when he asserts that, if life can proceed from the synthesis of the non-living, it is a thing of which he has no experience—is compelled to postulate a miracle; because no force of which he knows can span that tremendous gap between lifeless matter and living matter. Even in regard to matter itself, when asked to explain its origin, he must

L

either admit the occurrence of a miracle or cloak
his difficulty under a euphemistic phraseology.
No man of science, when confronted with some
startling phenomenon, in favour of which there
was strong evidence, would be ashamed to say,
"This is a thing which I should have never
expected, to me it is inexplicable; but perhaps we
shall one day know." In what respect, then, does
such an admission as this differ from what a
cautious theologian requires us to concede ?

But it is not enough to regard the Incarnation
by itself, and as an isolated event; it must be
considered in connection with the history—the
evolution, if the phrase be preferred—of humanity.
In the fullest sense of the words—now, if possible,
more fully than ever—it is the answer, God's
answer, to the earnest expectation of the creature,
to the "bitter cry" of humanity.

"O life as futile, then, as frail!" Do not these
despairing words express the feelings of many a
heart. Pessimism, of which we hear much, is no
new thing: it is not the mere outcome of an

unhealthy body or an unhealthy mind ; it expresses
a deliberate intellectual conclusion, in favour of
which there is very much to be said, if we regard
the present life apart from any hope of a future
and a better one,—for which, I believe, the case
actually grows stronger as man advances up the
scale of civilization and is raised, it matters not
how, above the animal world. Life's possibilities
are so great ; there is so much to do, so much to
enjoy in the nobler, not in the baser sense of the
word ; in this earth, both in its parts and as a
whole, there is such an inexpressible beauty, such
a boundless field of knowledge, were time and
opportunity only given ; in man himself there
are such potentialities of moral grandeur, yet such
endless disappointments, such constant failures.
Alike to love as to hate, to labour as to sloth, to
learning as to ignorance, to righteousness as to
unrighteousness, there comes one end. The old
pictures of the Dance of Death express an awful
truth. There, if in this life only you have hope, is
the picture-book of pessimism. Not to age only,

but to youth also : not to sorrow only, but to joy
also : not to failure only, but to success also : not
to vice only, but to virtue also, the grim spectre
comes, and leads away his helpless captive to
the prison-house of the grave, to the eternal
silence of the tomb. Vanity of vanities; all is
vanity !

If any one argued in this fashion in favour of
pessimism, what could be said against him ? Much,
I think, on the side of the animal world; not a little
also on that of the less civilized races of mankind ;
but I should feel that the difficulties of my case
increased in proportion as my estimate of my
client rose. There *are* jarring notes, there *is* a
discord in the harmony of nature; and these are
attuned, and can only be attuned by the Incarnation, which shows where promise has its per-
formance, where potentialities have their realization,
where failure is replaced by success. Man is ever
tormented by ideals which either mock him by
their evanescence or disappoint him by their failure.
In Christ the ideal is realized, and there is a living

union between the world of sense and the world of spirit.

Yet another deep-seated want of human-nature has been satisfied by the Incarnation. Man is a born idolater. The child and the savage can scarce conceive existence apart from form and material: they endow with some sort of vitality even the lifeless objects around them. The tendency of later years and of more advanced thought is to deify the human ideal and to people the celestial region with a crowd of divinities in human form. So strong is this innate instinct, that each spiritual type of religion has to wage a perpetual struggle for existence against reversionary tendencies. If, at any time, a great upward stride has been made by a leader of thought, his followers, instead of advancing onward, commonly step part-way back. This is true of Christianity itself, even in this nineteenth century; and in this land the faith of the majority is less spiritual than that "which was first delivered to the Saints." A God without boundary, without shape, without material, fails to satisfy a nature trained by the experiences of the finite. Man wants, man longs for the form which the eye can see, for the human heart which can beat in sympathy with his own. Unconsciously he reasons thus with himself: "What can a spirit know of my wants, my sorrows, my trials, and my temptations? My body is wrung by pain : that it has not felt. My passions struggle for mastery : this awful conflict it cannot understand. My life is dark with sorrow: that cannot come in the unchanging eternity. Talk not to me," thus the sufferer cries, "of these formless, changeless, abstract Powers. Give me that which can feel with me and for me in this weary and bitter conflict of life!" Jesus answers, "Lo, I come! I have borne the burden of humanity. I have felt its pains and sorrows! I have passed through its every stage from infancy to manhood. I have known its temptations, though not its sins. Art thou hated without a cause? They hated Me. Art thou persecuted for righteousness' sake? They persecuted Me. Art thou weary in well doing? I was weary too

Art thou bowed with sorrow? I wept by the grave of Lazarus. Art thou suffering bitter pains? I was wounded with the scourge and died upon the cross? Art thou in the horror of great darkness? Remember My agony in Gethsemane, and My cry on Calvary. Trust Me wholly, O faint-hearted one, for I know what thou dost feel. Trust Me wholly, for I gave My life for thee."

On former occasions I have striven to show that the irreconcilable antagonism between God and the universe, on which some have insisted, does not exist—that creation is the revelation of His wisdom, the manifestation of His power; that in every phenomenon—in the forces which regulate, in the light which illuminates, in the life which peoples the globe, we are beholding the action of a Divine energy, the revelation of the Unconditioned through the conditioned. In the Incarnation I recognize the crown and completion of the glorious work: the accomplished theophany: the perfect synthesis of the finite and the Infinite, in which the long series of types and analogues was realized, wherein

the "earnest expectation of the creature" received
that answer by which alone it could be satisfied !

> "Art thou weary, art thou languid,
> Art thou sore distrest?
> 'Come to Me,' saith One, 'and coming,
> Be at rest!'"

LECTURE V.

THE ATONEMENT.

"But God commendeth His own love toward us, in that, while we were yet sinners, Christ died for us. Much more then, being now justified by His blood, shall we be saved from the wrath of God through Him. For if, while we were enemies, we were reconciled to God through the death of His Son, much more, being reconciled, shall we be saved by His life."—Rom. v. 8-10 (R.V.).

"WHAT is man, that he should be clean? and he which is born of a woman, that he should be righteous?" That human nature is full of jarring notes, that in it noble aspirations and depraved tendencies are in constant conflict, is an awful fact, independent of any changes of opinion as to the meaning of the story of the Fall. Though the language of this appears to myself allegorical rather than historical, yet I consider original sin to be not only a theological dogma, but also an

M

induction from observed facts. That a discord
exists in human nature is a certainty. That it is
due to some past departure from a state of harmony
with the environment—which is only another
mode of expressing what is implied by the word
" Fall "—is highly probable.[1]

"All we like sheep have gone astray." From this
unwelcome conclusion there is no escape. As man
has advanced in ethical conceptions, he has only
realized more keenly his own imperfections and
failures; as he has pressed after an ideal, this, as it
became more clear in the brightening light, has
seemed to be yet further away, and to increase its
distance as he pursued.

The sense of sin becomes stronger as knowledge
grows. It is weak in savage man. He knows, like a
child, that he has to observe certain rules, the breach
of which entails penalties; but why this should be
he seldom asks. Commonly, like many a schoolboy,
he takes a merely mercantile view of an offence
and its penalty; the latter is the price to be paid

[1] "Old Truths in Modern Lights," pp. 269-286.

for the former, and so the affair is ended. His God is simply an invisible and very powerful chief; who, like a man, can be kept in good temper and appeased, but who generally is a rather good-natured personage. Demons, indeed, there are, whose intentions are malevolent; but the God on the whole is clever enough and kindly enough to keep these in check. So he goes through life in a schoolboy fashion—not, indeed, without April showers of tears, but with its sunshine too, and on the whole well contented with himself.

The same childlike brightness may be observed in the early history of Judaism. In peaceful times, when the spoiler came not, then every man sat under his own vine and his own fig tree, eating and drinking and making merry. As years went on the light grew stronger, but the shadows deepened. The soul began to long after God, the heart to realize its own bitterness—to know that no hyssop could purge its uncleanness, no blood of bulls and goats could wash away sin. Then came the Redeemer. Angel-voices proclaimed a message

of peace; but yet, though nineteen centuries have
almost passed away, and it has not been without
its influence in the world, we do but realize more
acutely than ever our own feebleness, our own
sinfulness.

But is there any other message which gives us
larger hopes ? As it seems to me, we are compelled, if we cannot accept the message of revelation, to this conclusion : There is in the ideal
world an absolute perfection; there is in the real
world an incurable imperfection. Between the one
and the other there is a great gulf fixed. This we
fain would cross, but it yawns too wide and too
deep.

The history of sacrificial rites, especially in their
later stages, is the history of man's effort to bridge
this chasm. In these, at the outset, the idea of
propitiation—the desire to obtain the favour of
the God—predominates; but it is gradually over-
shadowed by the idea of expiation, the endeavour
to avert the consequences of sin. Sacrifice, it must
be remembered, is not an institution of Jewish

origin. It is world-wide; the outcome of natural religion, not the result of direct revelation.

Yet another idea is prominent in all sacrifices involving the death of the victim, to which I shall have to refer in a later lecture—that there is an absorption of life through the blood, so that by means of it a communion in some sort is established between the God and the worshipper.[1] Such sacrifices, then, whenever and wherever performed, constitute acts of atonement; are admissions, however gross the conception, however unspiritual the idea, that the bond between the two parties has been weakened and requires to be strengthened, and so are indirect confessions of the frailty and sinfulness of man.

All Christians agree that the Lord Jesus, by His life on earth, made an atonement for the sins of mankind; that He became, by His death and resurrection, the living way across the great gulf which parts the realm of eternal death from that of eternal life. But we differ in the significance

[1] Robertson Smith, "The Religion of the Semites," lects. vi., viii.

which we attach to the atonement. In any endeavour to come to a conclusion on this question, we can hardly expect either direct help or opposition from the results of scientific inquiry, for we are dealing with matters which lie outside its province; nevertheless we may be aided by its methods, so as to test deductive reasonings from the words of revelation by the results of an inductive treatment of facts.

In meditating upon the significance of the atonement, we must be alive to the danger of an anthropomorphic phraseology. The employment of it is inevitable, because the relations of God to man can only be explained to us through the relations of man to man; nevertheless it may mislead us at every turn. For instance, such terms as "the wrath of God" or "the anger of God" may produce misconceptions. His wrath with sin is not emotional. It expresses the working of an eternal law—if the phrase be permissible—a severance and an alienation which are inevitable, which stand in the relation of consequence to cause. To give

a rough illustration : if I put my hand in the fire
and am burnt, I do not attribute this result to the
anger of the fire, or of nature, or of God. The
injury is the result of my action. That certain
antecedents should lead to certain consequences is
true in the moral as in the physical order. Sin is
the non-fulfilment of the Divine purpose ; man
had, man has, the power of choice, whether he will
obey the animal or the spiritual instinct.[1] As a
matter of fact, he hearkens sometimes to the one,
sometimes to the other; that is, he is never
without sin. But the sequence of consequence
and cause is a necessity of the Divine perfection.
" The seat of law is the bosom of God ; her voice
the harmony of the world." [2]

How, then, can man of himself escape from the
consequences of his wrong-doing? A disposition
to evil is a part of his nature. The doctrine of
" original sin," as expressed in the ninth Article of
our Church, in one aspect is only a special state-

---

[1] " Old Truths in Modern Lights," pp. 269–286.
[2] R. Hooker, " Ecclesiastical Polity," I. xviii. 8.

ment of the general law of heredity. The " infection of nature " represents in a phrase the results of observation; it is an induction rather than a dogma. Where the Scripture says, " All we like sheep have gone astray," " There is none righteous, no, not one," it is merely expressing an unquestionable fact. The man who asserted that he had never committed a sin would be regarded by common consent, even among the careless, as the greatest of self-deceivers; and if this be so, how, after having taken a poison, can we be delivered from its effects ?

It is not, then, so much *anger* which has to be appeased as the *natural consequences* of actions which have to be averted. A gulf has to be spanned. A gulf, we believe, has been spanned. In a higher sphere the independence of, the conflict between, personal will and natural law has been exhibited, with which we are familiar, in our humbler sphere, when we forgive the erring and accept the imperfect. God and humanity have been at one in the Person of Christ; in Him the law of righteousness is in harmony with the law of love.

But how are we to explain the effects of this act of self-sacrifice? Christians are agreed as to the fact of the atonement, but they differ much as to its significance. The Church of England wisely has not committed her members to any precise interpretation; affirming the fact, she leaves the appreciation thereof to the individual conscience.

Many solutions of the difficulty have been proposed, one or two of which I proceed to notice. Some have represented the atonement as a kind of bargain.[1] Man by sin sold himself into slavery. Satan had, so to say, a legal claim on him. So the Saviour offers Himself as a Substitute, and is accepted. But justice is satisfied in the letter rather than in the spirit; for it is known all along that the Victim will prove too strong for the oppressor. So it happens; the Captive bursts His bonds and tramples His captor underfoot. Another

---

[1] For an historical sketch of Patristic opinions, see Archbishop Thomson, "Aids to Faith," essay viii.

N

hypothesis may be briefly expressed as follows:
Man has sinned; God is wroth; some one must
suffer.   As I have heard it stated, "God must have
blood."   The All-loving Son comes forward as a
Victim, and exclaims, "Take Mine!"   He is slain—
"the Just for the unjust."   The Father's anger is
satisfied; He pardons, for the sake of One, the
many who have sinned.

Both these views we may unhesitatingly reject.
Supposing for a moment the principals in either
of the transactions were only men, we could not
affirm that they had acted up to a high ethical
standard.   But, in reply to such an objection, it
might be asked whether the verdict of our conscience can be trusted.   May not our ethical conceptions be vitiated by our imperfect knowledge?
My answer would be that they would err rather
on points of detail than on those of principle.   For
instance, we can seldom form an opinion as to the
justice or injustice of isolated occurrences; to our
limited view, God may often seem to deal hardly
with individuals.   For the explanation of this we

may be content to wait. We may also admit the possibility—the probability—that the moral sense of our race may become more acute, so that ethical standards are outgrown and a later age becomes dissatisfied with conceptions with which an earlier one was content.; but if we cannot trust the general accuracy of those ideas, which must be the basis of all our conduct, then right and wrong are reduced to arbitrary terms of only temporary value. So we may reject without hesitation both the above-named hypotheses as contrary to our elemental ideas of justice, righteousness, goodness, and refuse to attribute to God any course of action which we should, for ourselves, indignantly disclaim.

A third hypothesis, which has found very general favour, takes what is called a "forensic" view. The death of Christ procures the remission of our sins in this wise : The self-sacrifice and the perfect righteousness of Christ obtained what might be called a general pardon. Man admits his own guilt, but pleads the pardon. He is acquitted; he

is regarded as righteous because of Christ's
righteousness. This is like a fund upon which
man is empowered to draw in order to obtain his
freedom from a state of slavery. This, like the
festal robe bestowed by Eastern potentates, masks
and hides man's native squalor. For certain aspects
of this view there is much to be said. Its weak
point is indicated by the epithet "forensic"—that
is, by the effort to represent the manifestation of
God by the procedure of human law-courts; to
impose upon the Divine the limitations of humanity.
Thus, to myself, many of the disputes which
agitated the minds of the schoolmen and the
doctors of the Churches, reformed or unreformed—
disputes concerning "faith unformed" and "faith
formed," merit *de congruo* and *de condigno*—appear
to be mainly academic, originated by the attempt
to express through an imperfect terminology ideas
which refuse to be thus limited and trimmed.

If we were content to work in theology as we
do in science, and to admit that a definition may
be accurate or a principle sound for all practical

purposes, and yet be incompetent to withstand the rigid application of a "destructive sorites," or some other logical device, we should soon see that many difficulties were, like the Brocken spectres, only projections of human personalities on the mists of the unknowable.

But it is easier to perceive the defects in explanations than to amend them. We may refuse to admit the possibility of a divergence of Mind between the Father and the Son, or to attribute to the former a blind wrath which demands a victim, it matters not how innocent. We may be justly dissatisfied with those modifications of the last hypothesis which substitute a law for God, and discuss its requirements and its penalties, and yet we may feel that the matter is too great for our strength. So, if I were asked to state in precise language a theory of the atonement, which should at once be consistent with the words of Scripture, with our own sense of right and justice, and with the requirements of logic, I should not be ashamed to confess my inability. As well might we endeavour to wing our way through space to distant planetary systems, as to measure the immeasurable and to comprehend the incomprehensible. We can hope at the utmost to discover analogies, to approximate to the unattainable; and here, though we cannot enter perfectly into the seeming reconciliation of law and of love, we can learn the lessons of the life and death of Him Who was Son of man and Son of God.

Let me touch, in conclusion, upon one or two of these, for by them alone we can hope to gain some partial knowledge of that which must ever remain a mystery. Jesus bore the full burden of human nature. In His life and death He shared its pain and sorrow. Think of Him, weary and outworn, scorned and rejected, tortured and degraded by the long agony of the trial and the cross; cut off in the flower of His age and the fulness of His work; crushed by the sense that God would not, or even —if one may dare to say it—could not, help Him, and that wrong was stronger than right. No mourner, no sufferer, no martyr, hereafter could murmur, could despair. Needs must be that He should die, because until death writes the closing word on the page of each man's history, life's opportunities, whether for good or for evil, are not exhausted, and it is possible, in the weakness of age or in the pains of death, to fall from the way of righteousness. Needs must be that He should die; for if not, there would have been one trial through which He would not have passed, so that it could not have been said, "One of ourselves has borne all, suffered all, and triumphed over all."

What encouragement would it have been to us if the victory had been won in a nature other than our own? What boots it to tell me of the triumph of one who cannot feel my weakness? If I were in pain and you were insensible to pain, what lesson would it read me that you were cheerful and contented with your lot in life? But Christ took upon Himself a human nature, and we, erring, feeble, sinful beings, are at once nerved and shamed by the example of the one unfallen, perfect, sinless Man.

Yet more, let us take a somewhat wider view, and regard the sacrifice of Christ in the light of certain modern philosophies.[1] These tell us that the order of nature is the manifestation of the "will to live." If so, the physical universe is the expression of an energy acting, as it must always do, in accordance with unalterable laws. It follows, then, that we ourselves are but an aspect of this will; our brief portions of life, only its temporary individualization. But would that be a complete history of humanity? Are you prepared to accept the consequences of this theory, and live, as you should do, as expressions of this will alone? Gleams there are of something else, broken and shadowed though they be, which, though they interrupt the harmonious consistency of your philosophy, give to life all its tenderness and its brightness. Not only the "will to live," but also the "will to love," is manifested in this world, and it is written in largest, plainest characters in the life and death of Jesus.

If we can believe, as the majority do, that the

[1] Those of Schopenhauer and Von Hartmann.

person of every man indicates the action of volition as well as of mere vitality, so we may believe that in the Divine personality of Christ the two wills, that of "to live" and that of "to love," were exhibited in their temporal conflict and their eternal harmony.

It must never be forgotten that the atonement was not merely a single episode. It did not last, as we are apt to think, only from Gethsemane to Calvary. The hours of the Passion were but its completion. It began at the manger of Bethlehem; it was wrought in the daily life at Nazareth and in the homeless wanderings, by the shores of Gennesaret or in the deserts of Judæa, on the hills of Galilee and in the streets of Jerusalem. It was, in short, not only the "dying of a death," but also the "living of a life." Of this Christ bore the daily strain. Bore, not only its pains and sorrows, but also its petty cares, its little trials—those thousand trifles which in ourselves, like some destructive acid, too often corrode the more noble and indurate the more tender side of our nature.

o

He also bore that which is, for the more exalted spirits among us, the heaviest and most dangerous trial — misunderstanding and misrepresentation, injustice and ingratitude. In a word, He bore the whole burden of human life, without a murmur, without a falter, without a fall.

This, then, it is which constitutes the magnetism of the cross: "I, if I be lifted up, shall draw all men unto Me." Crushed by the sense of our own sinfulness, realizing that our own life is a failure, then we can feel the truth of these well-known words—

> "Nothing in my hand I bring,
> Simply to Thy cross I cling;
> Could my tears for ever flow,
> Could my zeal no languor know,
> All for sin could not atone,
> Thou must save and Thou alone!"

Do we require to formulate a theory of the atonement in terms of logical precision? As it appears to me, this is not only needless, but also, since the Divine relationships are beyond our comprehension, certain to bring us, by deductive processes, into positions which can be made untenable by inductive reasoning. That man's nature is a battle-field for opposing principles, is a fact; that even where the better prevails, the worse has won its partial successes, and the victor is more or less crippled, is a matter of daily experience; that the desire of making amends, the principle of sacrifice, is an instinct of human life; that man cannot atone for himself, is rendered almost self-evident by the fact that all ethical advance only enables him to realize more completely his own imperfections; that there is no motive moral force equal to that of perfect unselfishness; that there is, even in human forgiveness, inexplicable as it may seem, an actual alleviation of the burden of wrong-doing, and a power of exceptional strength in impelling the penitent towards a nobler goal, and in lifting him up to a higher plane of life;—these we may hold as axioms. In the words of Scripture we may see the expression, now of the one, now of the other, and yet may decline to attempt to co-ordinate them into a systematic whole, which shall appear logically complete in all its parts, because experience has shown that the narrowness of the field which can be commanded by our powers of observation must result in a disproportion of statement, and our efforts at precision must end in the accurate expression of mistaken notions. This, however, is not a peculiarity of theology; it is just as common in science whenever elaborate generalizations are founded on insufficient data, or precise definitions are attempted of that which is imperfectly understood.

This much, however, I think we may say. By the sacrifice made in the person of man—why and wherefore I do not venture to inquire—man's endeavours are accepted as if they had been perfected. We are dealt with as we are wont to deal with others. Do we require or expect in earth's dearest relations an absolute perfection? No; we bear and forbear. We accept the imperfect efforts, the incomplete results; we take, as we say, the will for the deed, provided that will has been honestly manifested in action. "She hath done what she could"—these were Christ's words to one who sought to do Him honour; these are now God's words of welcome to repentant humanity.

Love and justice unite in heaven as they are united on earth; as they were brought into perfect harmony in the Person of Jesus Christ, Who could abhor the sin and yet love the sinner, Who could condemn the guilty and yet forgive the penitent. If the Incarnation brought down heaven to earth, there is a sense in which the Atonement took back earth to heaven. In the one, as in the other, righteousness, love, and effort now form an eternal trinity in unity. Henceforth we are "persuaded, that neither death, nor life, nor angels, nor principalities, nor powers, nor things present, nor things to come, nor height, nor depth, nor any other creature, shall be able to separate us from the love of God, which is in Christ Jesus our Lord."

LECTURE VI.

THE RESURRECTION.

"Some said, What would this babbler say? other some, He seemeth to be a setter forth of strange gods: because He preached Jesus and the resurrection."—Acts xvii. 18 (R.V.).

MORE than eighteen centuries since the cross of Christ was an offence to the Jewish patriot, His resurrection to the Gentile philosopher. History repeats itself, and modern thought still recoils from accepting a doctrine which was derided at Athens and explained away at Corinth. To a Jew, the possibility of a resurrection, the hope of a resurrection, was in no way startling. To him the idea had long been familiar when Paul began to preach; for it was one of the chief subjects of debate between the two great schools of theological thought into which his nation was divided; but it was strange to Greek and to Roman, for though not a few of them believed in the immortality of the soul, they never hoped for a restoration of the body. It seemed to them, as it often does to us, a thing incredible "that God should raise the dead." The evidence of our senses, the evidence of experience, is totally opposed to it. "Dust to dust, ashes to ashes," that is their verdict on the body; as for its "guest and comrade," the soul, we can neither affirm nor deny that it may continue to exist.

At the present day, as I have said, the doctrine of the resurrection is a stumbling-block to many. By some it is denied, by others it is explained away, by still more any definite expression of opinion on the subject is nervously shunned. It may, then, be well that I should state at the outset two matters, of which, whether we like them or not, we are bound, as lovers of truth, to take account.

This is one: The resurrection of Christ was regarded by St. Paul as the cardinal fact of Christianity. This, we may fairly say, he made prominent in his preaching before the middle of the first century, when the event itself was as near to him as the Franco-German War is to ourselves at this moment. This is the other matter: The resurrection was not a dream of St. Paul's imagination. He refers to it as to a thing commonly believed among Christians. No trace of any rival story can be found. The alleged conflict between the Pauline and Jacobean versions of the Christian history is an hypothesis unsupported by a particle of real evidence, and may be dismissed as one of the cloudland creations of a class of critics who are more conspicuous for patient and laborious research than for their inductive treatment of its results. Nineteen centuries since St. Paul would have said—and the words, however we may mislike them, are just as true now—that Christianity without a risen Christ is no Christianity at all. It is only a system of ethics, inculcated by a life, dubiously historical, which obviously led to results so disastrous to the individual as to be most discouraging to future imitators.

But in regard to the historical fact of the resurrection of Christ—which, as St. Paul justly states, is the only valid assurance of the future resurrection of individual Christians—I do not purpose to say more to-day than to emphasize its importance. It has been a frequent subject of discussion during the last few years, and there is no hope of obtaining additional information. The alleged facts, the difficulties on both sides, are before us, and we must make up our minds. So I will not attempt to add to what I have already written,[1] but will only reiterate (for this, I think, is sometimes not clearly seen) that the Gospel story is either substantially true or a poetic legend, and that no opportunity is given us for halting between two opinions.

My remarks, then, on the present occasion, will be restricted to the doctrine of the future resurrection of the body, to which the Church Catholic is committed, not only by the so-called Nicene Creed,

[1] See "The Gospel of St. Paul," in "Old Truths in Modern Lights," p. 187.

P

but also by that older and simpler symbol which
bears the name of the Apostles' Creed. But in regard
to this we must not forget that there is much more
room for diversity of opinion. About an event which
is future we can know but little. Hence we must
expect that the sense in which the words affirming
a belief in the resurrection of the body are understood will vary greatly in different ages, for it will
depend upon the state of current thought. Thus
no interpretation of them, however popular it may
have been at particular epochs, can be regarded as
final and authoritative.

Obviously, in regard to the future resurrection
we cannot know more than we have been told. In
this case also we are obliged, as I have already
pointed out,[1] to take as axiomatic the possibility of
a revelation, and to assume that one has been made.
But even when this has been done, the instances of
a resurrection from the dead, which are on record
in the books regarded as authentic, do not really
tell us much, because they occurred under circum-

---

[1] Page 13.

stances very different from those which will attend the future resurrection. We find St. Paul's own belief stated with great fulness in the well-known section of his First Epistle to the Corinthians.[1] In this he combats doubts—probably the earliest doubts—which had been expressed upon the subject among Christians. His words are not less remarkable for their logical force than for their poetic beauty. The difficulties felt more than eighteen centuries since in Corinth were the same that are felt in London now. They may be gathered under two heads; the one, to which I have already referred, "Did Christ really rise from the dead?" and the other, which I purpose to consider at greater length, "How can this body be restored, after it has been resolved into its constituent elements, after it has been mingled with the dust, dispersed by the winds and waves, incorporated into we know not how many other bodies?" This question St. Paul answers by his famous analogy of the seed and the plant. Let us examine it a little

[1] 1 Cor. xv. 12-58.

more closely, remembering that the author makes
use of it as an analogy only, so that we are not entitled to insist upon a rigid interpretation of every
detail. It is needless for me to quote the words—
a poem in prose—in which St. Paul answers the
question, "How are the dead raised, and with what
manner of body do they come?" I may assume
them to be known to all; to most of us they have
spoken comfort and hope in our hours of deepest
sorrow. St. Paul, then, by his use of the analogy
of the seed and the plant which springs from it, to
represent the present body and the resurrection-
body, indicates something very different from the
ideas which have often been entertained by individual Christians, and to which the Church is
supposed to be so completely committed, that if
the latter be held up to scorn and ridicule, this is
deemed sufficient hopelessly to discredit the former.
What, then, are the facts, so far as known at the
present day, in regard to the development of a seed
—such as a grain of wheat—into the plant? Stated
concisely, they are these. The actual germ of the

future plant, very shortly after the fertilization of
the rudimentary seed, consists of an extremely
minute cell. This develops and increases by subdivision during the process of ripening, but the
aggregate to the last is small in size compared
with the whole body of the seed, and is very rudimentary in structure compared with the future
plant. In the next stage of its development—say,
when it is buried in the ground—the larger part of
the seed, that which envelops the embryo and is
the more conspicuous, disappears. As a matter of
fact, it is partly utilized in the sustenance of the
embryo, but to the ordinary observer it appears to
decompose, and be lost to sight like any other
residual organic structure. Then the new plant
protrudes from the ground, and in due course comes
to maturity. So, if we interpret St. Paul's analogy
strictly, we arrive at this result—that a considerable part of the original body (the seed) disappears; that almost the whole of the new body
(the plant), which has grown therefrom, consists of
totally new material, obtained and incorporated

from the earth, the water, and the air; that an
actual continuity between the two is maintained by
means of an organism which is very small in comparison with the seed, and is extremely minute in
comparison with the plant which has sprung from
it. This, then, the existence of a small link or con-
tinuous element, is the very utmost which we are
entitled to affirm in regard to the present body and
the "resurrection-body" of any individual, so that
gibes as to the difficulty of recovering the constituents of the former merely exhibit the ignorance of the mocker.[1] St. Paul does not assert, and
those who accept his guidance do not assert, that
any such recovery is needful to constitute a
personal identity of the individual in the present
state of existence and in that which is to come.

In this life the constituents of our bodies are
constantly changing; new material is being incorporated into them, old material is being

[1] The author referred to a lecture on "The Corruptions of the
Church," delivered not long before by the Rev. Dr. Momerie, in
which, according to the newspaper reports, this line of argument
was adopted.

excrcted from them. Between infancy and old
age possibly an entire, certainly a very large,
change takes place in the molecules of which an
individual body is composed, yet does this affect
the consciousness of personal identity? That is
the one fact of which each of us is more certain
than of anything else. It is, then, not necessary
that we should assert, and the Scriptures do not
assert, that the resurrection-body will be formed
of identically the same constituent molecules as
the present body; nay, St. Paul's words, when
fairly interpreted, are really opposed to any such
idea. He illustrates the relation of the two
bodies by that of the seed and the future plant,
which, as we have seen, have only a very slight
material connection, and differ altogether in
appearance and capacity, the latter being able to
discharge many functions which are impossible to
the former. Moreover, after calling attention
to the diversity in nature, both animate and
inanimate, St. Paul continues, "So also is the
resurrection of the dead. It is sown in corruption;

it is raised in incorruption: it is sown in dis-
honour; it is raised in glory: it is sown in weakness; it is raised in power: it is sown a natural
body; it is raised a spiritual body." In the verses
which follow he still further elaborates this contrast, and concludes by the emphatic assertion that
"flesh and blood cannot inherit the kingdom of
God;" so that a vast change must take place.
"This corruptible must put on incorruption, and
this mortal must put on immortality." Can anything be plainer than this? The utmost that St.
Paul's words, interpreted in their strictest sense,
can be made to imply, is the existence of some
very slight material connection between the one
body and the other—though, perhaps, even this
might be considered to be indirectly dispensed
with by the emphatic assertion of the necessity of
so great a change. The thing upon which St. Paul
insists as essential is a continuity of personal
consciousness.

But how is this continuity to be secured? Shall
we adopt the notion which was favoured by many

Jewish teachers about the time when St. Paul wrote, that there was a very small portion of the body—part of one of the vertebræ—which no force or agency could destroy, which remained intact and imperishable, the seed, so to say, which would one day germinate into the resurrection-body ?[1]   I fear this quaint fancy could be readily proved to be a fallacy, but we may find that it expresses a truth, though it be in an allegorical form.

As we have already said, the essential link between the two, or any number of, states of embodied existence is a continuity of consciousness.   It is the knowledge that "I am I" which constitutes personal identity.   How, then, is the continuity to be maintained after the death of the body ?   Is personal consciousness, as it were, for a time blotted out by death ?   Will the soul wake up on the resurrection morn, as one wakes sometimesfrom sleep, or revives from a swoon, without any sense of the length of time during which, so

[1] The *Luz.* See the Author, "Sermons on some Questions of the Day," pp. 107, 154; Edersheim, "Life and Times of Jesus," bk. v. ch. iv.

Q

far as we know, consciousness has been suspended? Or does consciousness continue without any break? This is a point on which very little has been revealed and nothing can be discovered; but such inferences as can be drawn from the Scriptures seem to justify us in giving an answer in the affirmative to the latter question. If this be so, consciousness obviously cannot be separated from life. But can we conceive of life, or at any rate of an individual life, as existent apart from a physical basis? I do not deny that such a thing may be, any more than I should deny that the waves of light are thrilling through the "black concave" from myriad suns even on the darkest night; but it can only exist in my consciousness, like the light, when it sets in vibration the atoms of the material. Nay, I admit that there is a Life, the great source and fountain of all personal life, an Energy which is the origin of all forces and a Power which is manifested in all matter; but the existence of this is to me an act of faith or a conclusion of transcendental reasoning. If I confine myself to the sphere with which my reason can deal, I can conceive of individual personal life only in connection with a physical basis, with matter of some kind.

Now, what is the first essential of a personal consciousness? It is the recognition that a difference exists between that which is of me and that which is not of me—between the "I" and the "not I." But by this a consciousness of boundary and limit is implied. What more do we require to constitute a corporeality? We indeed attach ideas of cohesion and solidity, more or less, to the word "body," but I fail to see that these are necessary. A consciousness of possession, a consciousness of boundary, seem to me all that is really requisite. We admit that in the present body the cohesion of its constituents is only a temporary one; if so, the magnitude of the time unit is surely a question of secondary importance. The life of an ephemeral insect may be as complete in its sensations as that of a creature which endures for a century. The question also, as it seems to me, is not affected by the physical condition of the body. Sensation with us is associated with certain stages of imperfect solidity in the material of the organism. But since the vibrations of light can pass alike through a sheet of glass and through the atmosphere, they might be regarded as affecting the one or the other in a very similar way, supposing for a moment we conceived a portion of each isolated from the rest and endowed like ourselves with sensation and reason—if we imagined a bit of the glass or a portion of the atmosphere capable of seeing; in such a case no serious difference would arise from the solid condition of the one or the gaseous condition of the other. Thus I find no insuperable difficulty in conceiving sensation to exist in an aggregate of matter whatever be its physical state. If, then, on any grounds, I believe in what is commonly called the immortality of the soul, and if, on scientific grounds, I am unable to conceive of the existence of life apart from a physical basis, I must suppose that after the destruction of the present body a body of some kind survives, invisible though it may be to

mortal eye, which, like the germ in the seed, constitutes a link between that which hath been and that
which shall be.

Is it not a suggestive fact that, in all matter of
which we know, the physical condition is a question
not so much of its nature as of its environment?
Gold is gold, whether it be solid, molten, or vola-
tilized; carbonic acid is carbonic acid, whether it
be gas, liquid, or frozen. Granted, then, that some
part of this bodily frame be perishable, there is no
à priori reason why another part may not depend,
for its physical condition, upon its environment,
and a great alteration in the one be the result of a
great alteration in the other.

Thus neither are the Scriptures nor is the
Church committed to the belief that the identical
constituent matter of the present body will be
resumed at the last great change. Of the details
of that wondrous process we know nothing. The
references made to it are obviously to be understood figuratively, not literally. We are not bound
either by the dreams and ideals of poets, painters,

and sculptors, or by the visions and fancies of holy men and women. The whole question, apart from a few simple statements, is an open one; concerning it we can only speculate, and the outcome of this must change in the process of time.

It might, however, be said that by the line of argument which we have been following we have not got further than a belief which has been very generally entertained, namely, that after the disintegration of the body a personality survives with which a material element may be associated; for in olden times it was commonly believed that the shades of the dead could be seen, though they could not be handled. The Christian doctrine affirms that a further change awaits this personality—the acquisition of a new organization—which may be termed a resurrection; though, as I have shown, an identity of its molecular constituents is not necessary, provided only there be an identity of personal consciousness.

But, as I have already pointed out, the physical condition of all substances is a question of environment; hence change in the latter may produce change in the former, or that which in one set of circumstances we should call disembodied, in another— speaking from the same standpoint—might become embodied. We are justified in being sceptical whenever we are asked to believe what is contrary to experience, but it is not safe to assume that our experience in this brief space of earthly life has exhausted the possibilities of the universe. Indeed, if experience alone were my guide, I should not believe in a future life at all; but if I am willing to admit that this is more than possible, I cannot, after going thus far beyond the limit which my experience prescribes, draw an arbitrary line, and refuse to make either room or allowance for the effects of a changed environment.

It is, however, possible that in this argument we may appear to be playing with the word "resurrection." You may say that a physical change in existing material would not suffice to satisfy the words of revelation, which demand the incorporation of new material. But why not? What would there be so startling in the assertion? In what is the body of every living creature at this moment occupied? In converting that which is not alive into that which is alive. My body, your body, takes in a quickening grasp the protoplasm which has lived, even the mineral salts which have not lived; it incorporates them into its structure. The process, indeed, is slow; it is balanced by one of disintegration and decay. But it is a fact, upon which depends our existence in this world as living sentient beings. By this process our present bodies have been built up; it was begun by a tiny germ. All the thought, all the ingenuity of man—the eloquence of a Demosthenes, the poetry of a Browning, the reason of a Newton—were once potentially present in a few cells of the simplest structure. This you admit; this, because it is of common occurrence, seems no miracle. Why, then, call us credulous when we believe that from the germinal self, after the destruction of the present body, an organism may arise far more perfect than this, and are not startled by the assertion that a process, similar to one which now occupies years, may be accomplished "in a moment, in the twinkling of an eye," when the old order passeth away and God makes all things new. In olden time, when the butterfly spread its new-born wings to the summer sun, men beheld in it, as in a figure, the completed history of the individual life. True, the analogy is an imperfect one; but it may well bid us pause before we insist that in the present we have attained to the utmost limits of our being, and deny the possibility of future change and development.

The body which shall be must differ greatly from the present one. In the eternal order there will be neither waste to repair nor destruction to arrest. The great enemy will not need to be combated by nutrition nor eluded by reproduction: thus most—in a sense, all—the present organization would be useless and superfluous, and so is not likely to reappear. But on this point it is idle to speculate. What we shall be, we know not. It is enough to be assured that in the better land there will be no

R

more weariness, but the delight of work which is not labour; no more pain, but the joy of perfect life; no more sorrow, but the bliss of unbroken peace and eternal love.

The resurrection of the body is no part of the order of nature, as we know it. Obviously it cannot be, but I have endeavoured to show that, so far from being wholly discordant from this order, we can recognize in it certain analogies even when St. Paul's words are interpreted with some strictness. Certainly it is a belief which we should not abandon with a light heart. Men sometimes talk as if the nature of our expectation was unimportant—whether it were of a disembodied existence (to use the ordinary phrase), or of a change which would develop the embryo, if I may so call it, into an organization far more perfect than this present one. It is not unimportant, and the general verdict of the human instinct supports my assertion. A belief in a continued personal existence is far older than Christianity. But when it signified merely the continuance of a shadowy "something"—which was the general expectation —did it satisfy? The wisest of philosophers could only say, "I go to die and you to live, but whether is better God alone knoweth;"[1] while the pages of Homer and Virgil[2] tell you what a poor substitute even the joys of the Elysian fields seemed for the solid realities of a life on earth.

But even these joys are only dreams. Put them aside. Put aside also the Christian hope of a future resurrection, and what yet remains? A choice between two opinions. Either the spirit may return to the God Who gave it, in the sense that the tiny portion of Divine energy, localized for a time in an aggregate of material particles, once more returns to the Great Source—the drop falls back into the fountain, the river is emptied into the ocean—and though the soul cannot be said to die, all personal consciousness, all individuality, is lost; or else there is nothingness; the latter, speaking from the standpoint of science, is the more probable, is the only reasonable alternative if we

---

[1] Socrates.   [2] "Odyssey," bk. xi.; "Æneid," bk. vi.

reject the voice of revelation. This, then, is the end: "To lie in cold obstruction, and to rot;" to vanish like the baseless fabric of a vision, and "leave not a rack behind." If this life be all, we of all God's creatures are dealt with most hardly. We have wearied ourselves in vain, we have worn ourselves out in the pursuit of unattainable ideals. "Let us alone!" we may well exclaim with the Lotos-eaters—

> "Let us alone. What pleasure can we have
>   To war with evil? Is there any peace
>   In ever climbing up the climbing wave?
>   All things have rest, and ripen toward the grave
>   In silence; ripen, fall, and cease:
> Give us long rest or death, dark death, or dreamful ease."

This is one alternative. Hear now the other: "Jesus said, . . . Thy brother shall rise again. . . . I am the Resurrection, and the Life: he that believeth on Me, though he die, yet shall he live: and whosoever liveth and believeth on Me shall never die." In which creed shall we trust, in which hope shall we labour, in which expectation shall we die?

LECTURE VII.

THE SACRAMENTS.

"Except a man be born of water and of the Spirit, he cannot enter into the kingdom of God."—St. John iii. 5.

"Whoso eateth My flesh and drinketh My blood hath eternal life; and I will raise him up at the last day."—St. John vi. 54.

FEW indeed are the societies what are not distinguished by a ceremony of initiation and a symbol of membership; the one is essential as a preliminary to the other. In each there must be some outward form, in each there is some hidden meaning. The form may be of the simplest, such as the signature of a name, or the participation in a common meal; but the one indicates submission to rule, however slight it may be; the other is a privilege enjoyed only by members.

Sacraments occupy this position in the Church

of Christ. The name is older than Christianity.
The Latin word *sacramentum* denoted primarily
a deposit—a sum paid into court, as we should
now say, at an early stage, by the disputants in a
lawsuit. This deposit, in the case of the loser,
was forfeited and applied to certain sacred uses.
The word also signified the military oath which
was taken by a recruit after enlistment. As the
earliest Christian terminology had a Greek origin,
sacramentum was not used in an ecclesiastical
sense till after Apostolic times, when it was
taken as the equivalent of μυστήριον (mystery) in
the other language. Employed at first, like this
word, in a wide sense, it was gradually restricted,
till at last, in most of the Reformed Churches, it has
been applied to two rites only—that of initiation,
and that which is the privilege of full membership.
The restriction is a question of definition. All,
however, will agree that Baptism and the Supper
of the Lord claim the highest place among sacraments, and most would admit that they alone
fulfil the definition of a sacrament which is

adopted by our own Church, namely, that it is "an outward and visible sign of an inward and spiritual grace given unto us, ordained by Christ Himself, as a means whereby we receive the same, and a pledge to assure us thereof." To these two, therefore, I shall limit myself on the present occasion.

Unhappily the prediction, "I came not to bring peace upon earth, but a sword," has proved no less true in regard to the sacraments than in other respects. The significance of these rites, apparently so simple, has been a battle-ground of opposing parties. The water of Baptism has kindled rather than quenched the fire of discord; the most expressive symbol of Christian union has become the most conspicuous sign of Christian dissociation.

Why this has happened, it is not difficult to understand. Every religious system, every attempt to bridge the gulf between the finite and the infinite, exhibits, more or less, a conflict between two antagonistic ideas. These are the magical, which in practice, if not in theory, makes the shaman, or wizard-priest, the master of the Divinity;

the spiritual, which makes him the servant or interpreter. In the process of revelation, whether indirect or direct, the one idea is replaced by the other; the centre of force is, as it were, shifted from the thing created to its Creator.

The history of Christianity, like that of Judaism, is the history of a struggle between these irreconcilable tendencies. The spiritual, on the whole, has prevailed over the magical, but the fight is waged with varying fortunes. Positions are taken and retaken; the advance is slow, and it may be that the victory will not be won before the day of earth's æons be ended.

In discussions relating to sacramental doctrines, scientific methods or scientific habits of thought might seem at first sight to be out of place. They might be deemed excluded by the phrase "a spiritual grace," which forms an integral part of our definition. But, as I venture to think, both in these questions and in those which we have yet to consider, they can play a more important part than many would be willing to acknowledge. This

I affirm for the following reasons : First, that in all scientific investigations clearness of thought and accuracy of expression, as far as possible, are deemed to be of the highest importance. But in many theological controversies, and especially those relating to the sacraments, which at the present time are distracting our own Church, an onlooker cannot fail to be struck with the difficulty of ascertaining what the persons who claim to be the supporters of high sacramental views really mean by what they say or what they do. The doctrine of Rome we know, whether we like it or not; the doctrine of the Church of England, though conveyed by expressions which sometimes admit of more than one interpretation, is, at any rate, very different from that of Rome; but in the present disputes it seems hopeless to ascertain whether the real question at issue is one of æsthetics and archæology, or of doctrines which are much nearer to those of the Roman than to those of the English Communion.

This is another reason. Experiment, which is

s

a process strictly scientific, has its place in ethical
theology. "By their fruits ye shall know them"
is not less true of theories than of men. Time
puts them to a test, and history records the results,
of which man is bound to make an inductive use.
If a certain dogma has been always the parent of
superstition, if particular kinds of authority have
been always abused, it is in the highest degree
improbable that the one can be true or the other
legitimate.

Questions like these must be investigated in a
spirit strictly scientific, without passion, fear, or
favour, with no other aim than to arrive at truth,
whether it accord or not with preconceived
opinions. This, however, if we may judge from
experience, is not usually the spirit in which
theological investigations are undertaken.

There is yet another reason. In all questions
our last appeal is to the words of Scripture. But
it is often necessary, in order to understand these,
to enter fully into the thoughts of the age when
the revelation was made; otherwise we may be

startled by phrases which, nineteen or more centuries since, would have seemed quite natural; we may construe literally words which then, as a matter of course, would have been understood figuratively. Thus Christian theology cannot be dissociated from the history of heathen thought and even of heathen superstitions, and the light of truth becomes more clear by the very contrast with the shades of error.

In this spirit, then, I shall venture to make a few remarks on the views which have been held as to the two great sacraments. The question which lies really at the root of all controversies may be stated bluntly—perhaps, to the minds of some, even offensively—in these words: Are they in any way magic rites? This is what is really meant by theologians when they ask, Are the sacraments means of grace *ex opere operato*, from the mere fact of their administration? In seeking to answer this question we must look not only at the history of their institution, but also at various general considerations, such as the state of thought at that time. It cannot be settled by the quotation either of isolated texts from Scripture, or of extracts from ecclesiastical authors. It is necessary to be sure that we understand the former right, and can trust the latter. The opinion of a good man who lived—say a thousand years ago —is not on that account of any more value than that of a similar man who is now living, unless we can show that he had better means of arriving at the truth. Authority has its place both in theology and in science, but it must not be allowed to preclude investigation in the former any more than in the latter.

Time does not permit of my attempting to trace out the effects of the Greek Mysteries in developing the outward ceremonial and the inner meaning of the Christian sacraments, but, as I stated in an earlier discourse,[1] the influence, for good as well as for evil, of Greek philosophy upon Christian theology—a subject which has been investigated with so much learning by the late Dr. Hatch in

[1] Lecture I.

his "Hibbert Lectures"[1]—must never be forgotten.

First, then, in regard to the sacrament of Baptism. Is it anything more than an initiatory ceremony? The view of the Church of England is expressed in a conspicuously cautious and guarded statement in the twenty-seventh Article, from which I imagine few would be found to differ. But the Jews were not singular in augmenting the law by tradition. Many Churchmen also desire a *Mishnah* as a hedge about the *Torah*, so that baptismal regeneration has been a frequent subject of heated controversy. On the last occasion, which some of us can remember, the Church of England was in danger of being rent asunder, though, as was subsequently remarked, neither of the disputants had defined what he meant by the term.[2]

"Baptism," it has been well said,[3] "is the oldest

---

[1] I do not mean to express agreement with every conclusion at which the author arrives.

[2] Remark by Bishop Thirlwall, quoted by Dean Stanley in "Christian Institutions," p. 10.

[3] Idem, p. 6.

ceremonial ordinance that Christianity possesses ; it is the only one which is inherited from Judaism." Immersion of the body in water—and in olden times this, not aspersion, was the mode of baptism —is naturally symbolical and suggestive of purification. This rite, so simple yet so significant, was appointed by the Saviour as the mode of initiation into the ranks of His followers. The plunge beneath the water was the symbol of a passage from a state of sin to a state of holiness, of a new birth by the action of the Holy Spirit. But though Jesus said, "Except a man be born of water and of the Spirit, he cannot enter into the kingdom of God," the words do not necessarily affirm that the rite, of itself, has any efficacy. He had just told Nicodemus that a new birth is needful for entrance into the kingdom of God. The phrase, apparently, was understood by the hearer in a literal sense ; it was intended, so the Lord explains, to indicate a spiritual change. Now that baptism in infancy has become the general practice, we are apt to forget that in early times the sacrament was usually received by those who were fully conscious of its significance and of their own responsibilities. It completed and rewarded a period, often long, of probation and preparation. In such case, to say that the rite was a means of special grace was not to attribute to it any magical power; it was to say no more than that for special ends special means are ordained. Christ has founded a Church; He has appointed a particular mode of joining it, has promised a special grace to its members. It were, then, the height of presumption in man, when his Master's charge is clear and definite, to say, "No, I will demand a grace on my own terms." Every society has its rules, and the advantages which it affords are conditional on compliance with these. But can the ceremony of itself work a change in the nature? We need not hesitate to answer in the negative. On the one side, to speak figuratively, is the faith of man; on the other, the Spirit of God. The rite does but complete their union, and set, as it were, the seal to an agreement which has been for some time in preparation. But, it may be asked, if this be so, is not the baptism of infants indefensible? We may reply that the sacrament is administered to them because it appears to have been the practice from the first to regard the household as represented by its adult members, and to receive the children together with the parents. Thus it seems natural to admit the children of Christian fathers and mothers into the Church of their parents at as early an age as possible. We may go even further, and say that the admission of the infant, in consequence of the desire and faith of others, bears witness to the solidarity of the Christian body; for in it, though the wants and responsibilities of the individual are never overlooked, it is always specially impressed upon him that he is one of a vast brotherhood, of the Church militant and the Church triumphant, the mystical body of Christ.

I could not, however, affirm that the word "regeneration" is to be understood in the same sense in the case of an adult and in that of an infant. What in the latter is in the germ, in the former is in the flower. The baptized infant has been made a member of the Church of Christ. Man has so far done what is his part. How the germ of life may develop, how the Holy Spirit may work, we will not curiously inquire. What might happen, did the infant die unbaptized, is not for us to determine. This only I will confidently affirm, that no fancied logical necessity, no possible interpretation of any obscure passage in Scripture, shall ever shake my trust in the justice and in the love of God.

In regard to the Eucharist opinions are yet more varied. It is impossible in a few minutes to discuss a controversy which for centuries has exercised the thoughts of earnest seekers after God. I shall, therefore, content myself with trying to put before you one or two ideas which have been brought, as it appears to me, into stronger relief by the investigations of our own time.

First, then, as regards the view maintained by the Church of Rome, commonly called Transubstantiation. I pass over the grosser forms of the

T

doctrine, which would be repudiated by the more thoughtful members of that Church—though the fact that they exist, and have been dealt with tenderly rather than sternly by its authorities, indicates that the dogma has a dangerous side—and content myself with noticing what I believe to be a fair statement of Roman Catholic opinion. It is that in the Eucharist the *accidents* of the bread and wine remain unchanged, but the *substance* of them is changed into the substance of the risen body of Christ. This definition, however, postulates that in an inanimate object—for brevity, let us say bread—there is, apart from its accidents, namely, taste, smell, consistency, form, chemical composition, and the like, a something—the substance or hypostasis—namely, that which makes it what it is. But is this more than a metaphysical figment? Is there any such thing as a pre-existent concept of bread? We apply the term to a certain aggregate of accidents; we extend or contract it, according to circumstances. Let us take an illustration. The pillars in a building within a furlong of this place are granite.[1] But what is granite? Simply a term which connotes a certain group of minerals, with certain mutual relations. The one and the other admit of modification within limits, but these limits are settled by the necessities of thought at each particular epoch, and we all know that cases exist where it is doubtful whether the rock ought to bear this name. The *hypostasis* of granite has a relative, not a real existence. It is only the epitomized expression of a group of accidents. Suppose a distinction made among these, and a name affixed to the part separated, a new hypostasis has not been called into existence, but only a new connotation invented.

Thus the doctrine of transubstantiation appears to me to be founded upon a fallacy—that of giving personality to a thought, concreteness to an abstract symbol.

Next I may observe—and this applies not to the Church of Rome only—that to assert the actual presence of the risen body of the Saviour in the

---

[1] Referring to the Carlton Club in Pall Mall.

eucharistic elements (using words in their ordinary sense) seems like a contradiction in terms. The word "body" in our connotation appears to imply this limitation—that it cannot be in two places at once. Yet either this is asserted by certain doctrines of the Eucharist, or a something is meant to which the word body cannot be applied. The difficulty is not eluded by asserting that we are speaking of a spiritual body. An adjective cannot deprive a substantive of its inherent qualities. To be accurate, we should say that the Spirit of Christ is present in the eucharistic elements, not His spiritual body.

But, obviously, the doctrine of the Eucharist must be sought in the words of Scripture. Here, then, we have to ask first what the words actually were, and secondly, what light is thrown upon their meaning by contemporary thought, so far as we can ascertain it. The opinions of later writers have an historical value and a psychological interest, but they have no binding force. The opinion on such a matter of the men, say, of the ninth century is of no more value than that of the men of the eighteenth century. For questions of fact (and in these direct statements are included) we must go back to contemporary evidence; for questions of interpretation it is the business of each age to co-ordinate those of all its predecessors.

The words of institution, used by our Lord Himself, are reported in the Synoptic Gospels and by St. Paul. Briefly and in effect they are these: Of the bread the Lord said, "Take, eat; this is My body." Of the wine, according to St. Matthew and St. Mark, "This is My blood of the covenant, which is shed;" or, according to St. Luke and St. Paul, "This is the new covenant in My blood." On indirect references to the subject in other parts of the Apostolic writings we need not dwell, because obviously their meaning will depend on that of the above statements.

Here one may remark that the difference in the rendering of the second clause is adverse to a very literal interpretation of either. Suppose a number of expressions are used of the same thing, of which

most may be either literal or figurative, but one
must be figurative; then the latter, of necessity,
carries with it all the rest. Again, we may observe
that when these words were used the Saviour had
not risen from the dead, had not even died upon
the cross, so that His body was then as the body
of other men. This fact also seems adverse to a
literal interpretation of the phrases.

But there is one passage which greatly helps
towards an understanding of these mysterious
words. In the sixth chapter of St. John's Gospel
a discourse is recorded in which the Lord reveals
Himself as the "Bread of heaven," and concludes
by stating, "Except ye eat the flesh of the Son of
man, and drink His blood, ye have not life in
yourselves. He that eateth My flesh, and drinketh
My blood, hath eternal life." There is more to
the same effect, which it is needless for me to
quote; but you will remember that the phrases
were at once misunderstood, and that in regard to
them the Lord said to His disciples, "It is the
spirit that quickeneth; the flesh profiteth nothing :

the words that I speak unto you, they are spirit, and they are life."

It has been debated, I know, whether these words have any reference to the Eucharist. Obviously they have a wider import, but I cannot doubt that they include it.

To understand their meaning we must enter as fully as possible into the thoughts of the past, and in this we have been greatly aided by the comparative researches into ancient religions which have been pursued with so much success during the last quarter of a century. These are dreaded by some; to me they seem very helpful towards the right understanding of revelation; for, so far as we can discover, it is God's pleasure to lead mankind from darkness to light by using the materials which are ready to hand, to employ in the process of education current ideas and familiar thoughts, purging them from error, correcting their imperfections, making prominent the good—working, in a word, from the lowland towards the height, from the natural towards the spiritual.

What, then, appears to have been in olden time the essential idea in all sacrificial rites which involved the death of a victim? Not so much propitiation, though that was a very ancient notion; not so much expiation, though that sometimes was very prominent; but a communion of the worshipper and the God through the blood. "The blood is the life" is an idea older than Judaism. That to drink the blood and to eat the flesh was to share in the life, is a world-wide idea. It was the inner meaning of every sacrificial feast. By it the bond of union between the God and the worshipper was strengthened, for they became united, as we say, by a tie of blood.[1] Time does not permit me to enter into any detail on this interesting question—the history of the sacrificial idea; I must content myself with stating the general result. This, then, enables us to perceive the underlying principle both in Judaic ritual and in natural religions, of which the Lord, we may

[1] See especially Robertson Smith, "Religion of the Semites," lects. vi., viii., ix., xi.

venture to say, sought to avail Himself. It was
as though He said, " You must indeed be partakers
of a higher life, that which I bring unto you. The
ritual of the past has been to some extent misleading, because it is liable to be understood too
literally. My sacrifice fulfils all that sacrifices
hitherto have really typified. Take yet simpler
emblems—things without life instead of living
creatures; let them become the embodiments of
spiritual truths, the channel of spiritual realities."
Once more, as in all progressive revelations, there
was a consecration of the simplest means to the
highest ends.

Are these symbols only ? In one sense they are
nothing more; yet in another they are the means
whereby an energy, which is behind and beneath
the forces and the forms of the earth, is communi-
cated to one of its creatures; quickening that with
celestial fire, as the dull carbon glows at the
passage of the electric current; but they become
what they are by the faith of the recipient and
the operation of the Spirit of God. So it is in

U

prayer; it is not the place or the form of words which avails, but the cry of the soul. So it is in all that quickens the spiritual life. Rites and ordinances have their value—man, being as he is, cannot dispense with them; but he must remember that they are only steps in the ladder by which his soul ascends from earth to heaven, so that the top will not be reached more quickly by lingering to gaze at them.

Thus, in every sacramental ordinance, the ritual is unimportant, except so far as it is favourable to a reverential expression of prayer and thanksgiving. It may—to some extent it must—vary with the thoughts and the habits of the age, so that a ceremony is not good simply because it is ancient, and any one that favours the idea of incantation is rightly disapproved as misleading and dangerous. Nothing of this kind is sanctioned by the Church of England in its authorized formulæ. In the twenty-eighth Article a number of scriptural phrases are summed up by the statement that "the body of Christ is taken and eaten in the Supper only

after a heavenly and spiritual manner, and that
the means whereby it is received is faith." The
words "heavenly and spiritual " remove the communion altogether from the order of things
sensible. A presence of Christ, a communication
of Christ, there is, in and by the eucharistic
elements; but where is there not a presence, where
is there not a communion, where the heart is
expectant of Him, where the soul longs after Him ?
Not alone in the pillared aisle and beneath the
vaulted roof of buildings made with hands; not
alone amid the melody of music and the voices of
ministering choristers; not alone when the smoke
of incense rises and the priests bend low before
the altar; but there also, in the stillness of the
forest shades; there also, where the breeze blows
soft over the meadow-flowers; there also, where
the clouds drift lightly among the silent peaks.
Nay, but not only there; even in the busy haunts
of men; even in the hurry of the daily work;
even amid the roar of the crowded street. Christ
is there, whenever and wherever the soul longs

after Him. Communion with Him we need, if we would escape from the doom of all earthly things. If the soul is to live, it must be by the life which Jesus gives; if the body is to rise again, it must be by the power of His resurrection. This is a great mystery—that Pantheism which is really Christian; but grander far than all the circumstance of magic rites is the tremulous expectancy of the soul, as it awaits in silent awe the incoming of the Spirit of God, the wondrous operation of mighty spiritual forces. These thrill through nature and through man, till at last that which is corruptible doth put on incorruption, and that which is mortal doth put on immortality.

LECTURE VIII.

THE CHURCH.

" If he refuse to hear the Church also, let him be unto thee as
the Gentile and the publican. Verily I say unto you, What
things soever ye shall bind on earth shall be bound in heaven :
and what things soever ye shall loose on earth shall be loosed in
heaven."—St. Matt. xviii. 17, 18 (R.V.).

In the present day we hear very much about the
Church and Church authority—much more, indeed,
than did our grandfathers. Perhaps they heard too
little; perhaps we hear too much. Whether this
be so we will not at present seek to determine,
but we will try to ascertain as far as possible the
meaning of the terms. A process this which is
always important, for to many minds a sonorous
word or an impressive phrase presents great
attraction, and becomes a convenient cloak for
haziness of thought. A liability to this hypnotic

influence is so marked a weakness in the present age, that it would not surprise me if phrase-worship were reckoned by future historians as one of our national idolatries at the close of the nineteenth century. Science does not wholly escape it; politics are saturated with it; Christian societies are all more or less infected by it. Among certain of the last we hear, in sermons, speeches, newspapers, books, so much of the Church and Church authority, that we are bound to endeavour to ascertain the meaning. An effort to arrive at it inductively from the above-named sources soon lands us in perplexity. Sometimes it means a decision of a small local council in bygone ages, not seldom that of a little coterie at the present day; sometimes it means the opinion of an ancient author, more conspicuous for zeal than for learning; not seldom that of the editor of a partisan journal, who has no more right to represent even the Church of England than have I to speak for her Majesty's ministers.

It will, then, be my endeavour, in this concluding

lecture, to answer—though it must be in the barest outline—from the authorized formulæ of the Church of England, these two questions: (1) What the Church is. (2) What authority the Church claims. The word " Church," perhaps I should explain, signifies the Lord's house, and it is used when it designates a body of Christians, and not an actual building, as the equivalent of the Greek word *Ecclesia.* This signifies an assembly selected or summoned for a special, generally a legislative, purpose. In this sense the word is much older than Christianity, and was in common use at Athens. My remarks also, it may be well to add, refer to the Church on earth, or to the Church militant, as it is frequently called, and must often, for obvious reasons, be restricted to that branch of it to which we belong.

In the nineteenth Article we shall find an answer to the question, " What is the Church ? " This may be regarded as the deliberate opinion of the Church of England, for which alone she is responsible as a body corporate. It runs thus: " The visible

Church of Christ is a congregation of faithful men, in the which the pure Word of God is preached, and the sacraments be duly ministered according to Christ's ordinance in all those things that of necessity are requisite to the same." Obviously there are at least three phrases in this definition on which almost endless disputes might be founded ; namely, what is a *faithful man?* what is the *pure Word of God?* what is *due ministration of the sacraments?* These, however, we may avoid in all fairness, so far as our present purpose is concerned, by stating that it has never been the practice of the Church of England to favour the more rigid and exclusive interpretation of an epithet or a phrase, and that, as elsewhere shown, she does not deny to congregations, from which she is even compelled to separate, the right of membership in the Church of Christ.

Next, what authority, in the same formulary, is claimed for the Church ? It is affirmed, clearly though indirectly, that no Church is infallible, for it is said that even General Councils may err, and

have erred.[1] This admits that the authority is
constitutional, not despotic. But the Church
claims power "to decree rites or ceremonies, and
authority in controversies of faith."[2] This, however, is immediately safeguarded by a passage
which limits the authority by the Scriptures. The
Church must ordain nothing contrary to them ;
must explain no one part of them so as to make
it contradictory to another, and must not enforce
anything which is not found in them as an article
of faith necessary to salvation. The Church also
claims power to appoint, or ordain, persons to
preach in public and to minister the sacraments
in the congregation,[3] the power being exercised
"by men who have public authority given unto
them in the congregation to call and send ministers
into the Lord's vineyard." On this I will only
remark that while it is obvious how the latter
words are interpreted in practice by the Church
of England, she does not condemn explicitly other

---

[1] See Article XXI.   [2] Article XX.
[3] Article XXIII.

X

congregations of which the customs differ from her own.[1]

From the above statements it is clear that our Church does not claim, and the Church ought not to claim, more authority than is conferred upon it by the Scriptures. To what, then, does this amount? The controversy turns mainly on the meaning of the words which I have quoted in my text. We find them, or words similar to them, used on three occasions. These are: the personal promise to St. Peter, from which this authority to bind and to loose is sometimes called "the power of the keys;" the promise to the ten Apostles after the Resurrection, related in St. John's Gospel; and the promise to the Church or congregation—that is, to the whole body of Christians—which I have already read.[2] In order to save time we will speak mainly of the last, as being the most inclusive promise. What, then, is the meaning of the phrases "to bind" and "to loose," applied in this case

[1] Cf. Article XXXIV.
[2] Matt. xvi. 19; John xx. 22, 23; Matt. xviii. 17, 18.

and in that of St. Peter to things or precepts, in the case of the ten Apostles to remitting and retaining of personal sins ?

One thing we may be sure they cannot mean— they give no power of establishing an arbitrary standard of right and wrong. Right will be still right, and wrong will be still wrong, even though a Church or the whole Church were to declare to the contrary. Either a tacit limitation must be supposed, or a promise of infallibility be assumed, for which we cannot find any warrant elsewhere. But in reality any difficulty as to the meaning of the words is of subsequent origin. When first used they would be readily understood. Let me quote the words of a very competent authority: [1] " No terms were in more constant use in Rabbinic canon law than those of ' binding ' and ' loosing.' The words are the literal translation of the Hebrew equivalents—*asar*, which means to bind in the sense of prohibiting; and *hittir*, which means to

[1] Edersheim, "Life and Times of Jesus," bk. iii. ch. xxvii. (vol. ii. pp. 84, 85).

loose in the sense of permitting." They refer "simply to things or acts, prohibiting or else permitting them;" that is to say, they confer—as I have heard it well expressed—"the power of making bye-laws."[1] This power, inherent in all societies, but always limited by the charter or foundation-deed, here receives a solemn sanction. Penalties may be enforced, again within limits, for the breach of these bye-laws, and wilful contumacy may be punished by expulsion. If the Church has forbidden that which ought to be forbidden, then exclusion from the Church militant on earth means exclusion from the Church triumphant in heaven. If, on the contrary, she has bound that which ought not to be bound, the sin of setting up a false standard of right and wrong lies at her door. The individual conscience must be the ultimate judge; but it must be remembered that opposition to the body corporate involves the gravest responsibilities, and can only be justified

[1] In conversation, by a friend, now a professor in the University of Cambridge.

when a man, after calm deliberation, is convinced
that bye-laws have been enacted which are in
violation of the charter. In short, these words
confer exactly the same kind of power which is
possessed by all societies; they involve similar
responsibilities, both as to the individual and as to
the society, and they do not exclude the action
of the protestant or the reformer.

But it may be thought that the power conferred
by the words spoken to the ten Apostles, after the
Resurrection, goes much further: " Whose soever
sins ye remit, they are remitted unto them; and
whose soever sins ye retain, they are retained."
On this point I will not express any opinion of my
own, but quote that of Bishop Westcott.[1] "As [the
former] promise gave the power of laying down
the terms of fellowship, so this gives a living and
abiding power to declare the fact and the conditions
of forgiveness. The conditions, as interpreted by
the Apostolic practice, no less than by the circumstances of the case, refer to character. The gift

---

[1] Gospel according to St. John, xx. 23, *note.*

and the refusal of the gift are regarded in relation to classes, and not in relation to individuals. . . . It is impossible to contemplate an absolute individual exercise of the power of 'retaining;' so far it is contrary to the scope of the passage to seek in it a direct authority for the absolute individual exercise of the 'remitting.'"

No despotic power, then, is vested in either individuals or community; the gift of the keys of the kingdom of heaven does not permit bishop or priest, individually or collectively, arbitrarily to exclude from the kingdom of heaven in its wider sense. To claim this power is an arrogant and audacious usurpation; to concede it a base and immoral superstition. See ye to it, for such a power is claimed in parts of the Church of Christ; it is claimed nowadays by some in our own Communion. See ye to it. Our forefathers suffered and died for liberty of conscience; are we to be led back into bondage because we are too weak and sentimental to think for ourselves?

Further, it must not be forgotten that the power

to bind and to loose belongs, according to the text, to the whole Church. But it is usurped by one class, the clergy. How this came about, that it was almost inevitable, is a matter of history. Circumstances developed a dominant class—I had almost said a dominant caste—in the Church. It became an assumption that in matters spiritual it was the duty of the ecclesiastics to rule, of the laity to obey. Yet in these also, the latter, if otherwise qualified, have a right to a voice. Even in the Church of England some traces of this ancient mistake still linger, and the laity are far from possessing the power which properly belongs to them, or rather the relations of the two classes and of the Church and the State are a jumble so confused as to be marvellous even for England.

These claims on the part of the clergy are no new things; for centuries they were not only made, but in general conceded. In many lands and for long periods the sword of the State has been either grasped or guided by the hand of the ecclesiastic. Deal, then, with the claims in a scientific spirit;

apply the test of experiment. What has been the practical result?

If the authority of the Church extend to temporal power, then those countries where this has been possessed for centuries without dispute should be to the world patterns of righteousness, justice, purity, courage—in short, of every manly and Christian virtue. Will this be asserted of them by any impartial historian?

The Church has also claimed to be supreme in matters of learning and science—to hold the keys of the library and the laboratory. With what result? That clerical opinion—which in practice if not in theory has represented Church opinion—has almost invariably proved, in the long run, to have been wrong. For centuries the severest ecclesiastical censure would have fallen on any one who maintained that this earth was a globe, and the nonsense of Cosmas Indicopleustes was greedily swallowed. For centuries it was an unpardonable heresy to assert that the earth moved in an orbit about the sun. For centuries the door of the laboratory was closed, the path of experiment was barred; the writings of the Fathers, not the works of nature, were deemed the court of appeal in questions of science.[1] Not one branch alone of the Church has fallen into this error, nor is the tale only of other days. The Church of England, happily, has never placed herself in open antagonism to scientific progress, but the influence of her members has been commonly adverse, their actions have brought her much discredit.

How long is it since the geologist was denounced because he could not accept the Mosaic cosmogony as literal history? What happened when it was proved that the human race had occupied the earth for more than six thousand years? What happened when the hypothesis of evolution was first advanced?[2] From a hundred pulpits and a hundred platforms we were assured, not seldom by

[1] If any one feels disposed to deny this statement, I recommend him to read " The Warfare of Science," by A. D. White.

[2] It is needless to accumulate references. Two of these epochs are well within my own recollection, and I can remember something of the other.

Y

those who had not investigated, and were incompetent to investigate, the questions, that if this or that were generally accepted it would be the downfall of faith and the triumph of infidelity. Yet now both are regarded as questions merely scientific; both are accepted by many sincere Christians.

But why do I dwell on these things? Why neglect the maxim, "*De mortuis nil nisi bonum*"? Because even now very many persons, especially among the ministers of religion, will not honestly recognize the mistakes of the past, and the possibility of like mistakes in the present; because even the Church of England itself, while it has been wisely cautious in attempting precision of definition or in adding to dogmatic theology, has been, and still is, timorous in lopping off parasitic growths and parting with outworn garments; still does not recognize the mischief which can be wrought by zeal when divorced from discretion, and the absolute duty, however painful it may be, of withstanding even an Apostle to the face when he attempts to bind that which Christ has loosed.

We need in the Church the spirit which prevails among scientific societies. There also, as everywhere, nonsense is talked. But with this difference. Let it walk as delicately as King Agag, sooner or later there comes a Samuel who hews it in pieces before the Lord. Nonsense is nonsense by whomsoever it is uttered; the more mischievous in proportion to the speaker's goodness. Would that the rulers of the Church of England were a little less prone to decorous euphemisms and a little less afraid of the naked truth; that, in their tender compassion for the weaker brethren, they would occasionally remember that the strong also have their rights, and may become weary of a diet of milk—especially if it be sometimes sour !

The Church, like all other bodies of men, has made mistakes, grievous mistakes, in the past. Better acknowledge them frankly, for in so doing we shall be convinced of our own fallibility, and be made cautious of attempting to resume an authority which has been demonstrated by experience to be both unwarrantable and mischievous. The mistakes, the errors, were venial, were almost inevitable in the past; in the present day they are without excuse. Those who walk with their eyes shut must not expect when they stumble the pity which is extended to the blind. The Church of the first centuries was confronted with a problem of appalling magnitude and difficulty. It found itself standing, like Aaron, between the dead and the living; but what a death, what a life! Only those who know intimately the history of Rome and of Byzantium can realize the awful, the hopeless corruption of the dying Empire, which had ruled and ruined the civilized world. It was as though the vision of Patmos was being fulfilled, and the angel had cried to all the fowls that fly in the midst of heaven, " Come and be gathered together unto the great supper of God."[1] They had come to eat the flesh of kings, of captains, and of mighty men—barbarian hordes from the North and from the East; Goth and Vandal and Hun, Teuton and Northman and Slav, ignorant as children,

[1] Rev. xix. 17 (R.V.).

reckless as boys, but vigorous as men. On the one hand was the paganism of the "old *régime*," effete, trodden underfoot, but not extinct; on the other, the paganism of the invader in all its pride of strength and success. These the Church had to win, to mould, to humanize, to regenerate. What wonder if mistakes were made; what wonder if strength was matched by craft; if the rude barbarian was awed by mystic rites and pompous ceremonial, and the messenger of Christ was too prone to claim the powers of the magician? We may regret, we may take warning for ourselves, but we can scarce venture to blame, for even in this day few temptations are more subtle and more seductive than that of doing a little evil to bring about a great good. So do not think that I delight in decrying the men who fought this long fight. We of this age, in very truth, have entered into their labours. They gave up all for Christ. Who am I, living here at my ease, that I should censure an Ambrose or a Jerome, a Winfried or a Columba, an Augustine of Hippo or an Augustine of Canterbury, or any of that great multitude, whom no man can number, who suffered, laboured, and even died for Christ ?   I may admit the mistakes of a Benedict or a Francis, of a Xavier or a Loyola, of a Bruno or a Cuthbert, of a Fisher or a More, as I might do those of a Gordon or a Damien, and yet confess myself unworthy to be numbered with them. They loved much.   Let us try to imitate them in that. But to devise euphemistic names for error is not the way to advance the cause of truth ; to admit facts, even if they be unwelcome, is the duty of the Christian no less than of the man of science.

One thing the Church cannot do—that is, to recall the past or galvanize dead institutions into life. A flock submissive as sheep, docile as children, has been and still is the dream of a hierarchy.   It is a dream as fond as it is foolish. Progress, not reversion, is the law of healthy life.   When man attempts a renaissance, he is generally more successful in mimicking the follies than in imitating the virtues of his ancestors.   To reform is not only to return to ancient ways.   The clock of time cannot be put back; and it is no less true of a nation than of a man, that if an adult tries to play the child he generally succeeds only in playing the fool.

What power, then, has the Church? Is it a mere shadow of a shade? Far from it. In the first place it possesses, within the limits of its commission, the power of self-government. To disobey the ordinances of a Church is always to undertake a very grave responsibility; it is often to do very wrong. Only in extreme cases does the right of private judgment justify us in violating a definite law. Let me give an example, to make my meaning clearer. The Church of England forbids marriage in certain cases of affinity. Personally, I hold that in one of these the prohibition is a mistake; but as things are I should regard myself as bound by it. Again, there are two or three phrases in the Book of Common Prayer which I would gladly see modified or omitted; but I do not on that account feel justified in leaving them out at my own pleasure. In short—and this remark does not apply to matters ecclesiastical only—I do not regard it as a sacred duty to set myself above the law, nor do I feel the slightest sympathy for those apostles of the modern gospel of anarchy, whom the sound sense of our forefathers would have considered as common offenders, and the hysteric sentimentality of the present age regards as interesting martyrs.

Lest, however, I should be misunderstood, let me add that I do not admit the obligation of practices or regulations which have fallen into general disuse, unless good cause can be shown why they should be revived; for the becoming obsolete must be recognized as a virtual repeal, whenever the formal process, as is the case in the Church of England, notoriously involves great difficulties. For instance, whatever be the validity of the canons ecclesiastical, I feel no more bound to order my daily apparel by the seventy-fourth of these, than by the whims of clerical tailors or other leaders of fashions ecclesiastical in the present day.

Again, the Church possesses the power of a healthy public opinion. For good and for evil association is a mighty force. Divide and rule, unite and conquer, are commonplaces. The Church is a corporation pledged to war with evil and to advance good. It is the one human society where righteousness in thought, word, and deed is assumed to be the normal condition, and every departure from it abnormal. Whatever difficulties may beset the Christian in his path through life, however isolated he may appear to be, in distant lands, in uncongenial society, in thankless toil, he is nerved by knowing that, even in this outpost duty, he is no solitary Ishmaelite, but one of a mighty army, united in a common hope and a common strength, directed and led, though he beholds Him not, by the captain of the Lord's host, against whom no evil shall prevail.

There is yet a third power, connected closely with the last—the moral force of censure and of forgiveness. The former is felt, often keenly, even when it is known to be undeserved—nay, even when to incur it is a positive duty. It is dreaded, when merited, even by those who bluster most

z

noisily and affect a contemptuous indifference. To desire the praise of men rather than their blame is natural to every one—so natural that it is always a great temptation to prophesy smooth things when it is the time to speak out, to cry " Peace ! " when there is no peace. Great also is the power of forgiveness. At a certain stage in repentance, especially to a sensitive nature, it is very helpful to learn that the offence is forgiven by those who have been injured, because it is then felt that the rift is not past repair ; that the injury, though it cannot be recalled, may be at least effaced. A message of forgiveness is a message of hope. So the Church in her public capacity assures the truly penitent of that Divine pardon, of which all human forgiveness is but the reflection. So also she empowers her ministers, as ambassadors of Christ, to proclaim in special cases to the troubled conscience that the Lord is merciful, and will not turn a deaf ear to the cry of the contrite heart. They cannot tamper with the eternal laws of right and wrong; they cannot by magic rites

compel the gates of heaven to open to the unfit
and close against the fit; but they can bid even
the worst of sinners not wholly to despair, for they
speak in the name of Him Who listened to the
prayer of one justly crucified for his offences
against man and against God.

Looking back upon the past, are we not right in
saying that what the Church has bound and what
the Church has loosed, not as a hierarchy but as a
whole, has been confirmed by the verdict of God,
made manifest in history? Learn what the world
was in the days of the Cæsars, even of the Constan-
tines, and compare this with its present state.
Enlarge, if you will, upon every mistake and every
shortcoming; insist that, owing to them, the results
fall far below a legitimate expectation; still the fact
remains that a great change has passed over society.
Granted that the pastimes of Western Europe—
even of our own land—are sometimes brutal: they
were horribly cruel in the days of the amphi-
theatre; granted that the poor are still many
and miserable: poverty was far more hopeless

nineteen centuries since; granted that they are
still sometimes down-trodden: they were in utter
bondage then; granted that the rich are sometimes over-luxurious: wealth was far more wanton
then; granted that society is sometimes profligate:
what are nameless vices now were venial indis-
cretions in pagan Rome. Whose influence put a
stop to gladiatorial contests; mitigated and in
many cases abolished slavery; founded hospitals
for the sick and penitentiaries for the fallen;
insisted that the thrall, no less than his lord, had
a soul to be saved or to be lost? It was the Church.
Here and there ecclesiastics may have opposed and
thrown their influence into the wrong scale, but in
yet more cases they have been the leaders in
works of mercy and love. These results are the
results of Christianity and so of the Church; for
that means the whole body of Christians.

There is work enough to do in this nineteenth
century; there is a crisis coming which will tax
the energies and test the strength of every Christian man and woman. I will speak of our own

land and our own Church only, though the coming
struggle is one not thus limited. This is no time
for questions of vestments and ritual. These are
at best as the tithing of mint, anise, and cummin;
at worst, too often the remnants of old-world
superstitions, which are dying hard, as such things
always die. The message which we must carry
is, once more, of the very simplest kind. Let the
leaders of the Church, let the ministers of the Church,
boldly declare that it is a Church of growth and
progress, not of stereotyped immobility. Let
them proclaim the message of Christian righteousness to all—to the patrician and to the plebeian—
fearless alike of courtier or of mob. Let them bid
the rich man remember that wealth has not been
entrusted to him merely that he should be clothed
in purple and fine linen, and fare sumptuously
every day. Let them bid the poor man remember
that in giving bad work for good pay, in defraud-
ing his employer or tyrannizing over his fellows,
he is showing himself no better than the stock
subjects of his denunciation. This is an age of

shams—of shams commercial and shams moral—
worthless materials tricked up to look like useful
wares, and ugly vices cleverly clothed in the modest
garbs of virtues. To strip the mask from all alike,
from rich and poor, from aristocrat and democrat,
from the fraudulent and the impostor in every
rank, is the duty of. the Christian Church. In all
ages of windy words and frothy declamation, men
lose sight of principles of ethics and principles
of religion. Never was it more true than of
England in this age of irresponsible chatter and
foolish gossip, when the mass of men buy their
opinions ready made for a halfpenny, and distinguish virtue from vice at the bidding of an
unknown political partisan. To all this there can
be but one end. The path has already been trodden,
though under slightly different circumstances, by
not a few states. It is that of senile decay and
ultimate death.

Let Christians lay this to heart, for it is not yet
too late, so much is the good mingled with the evil
in the present age. Let them recognize the danger ;

let them cast aside political jealousies and partisan
hatreds; let them sink as far as possible even
differences of creeds, and stand shoulder to shoulder
in the army of Christ against the World, the
Flesh, and the Devil. If this be done, the victory
is sure, for on God's earth truth must at last prevail;
nay, the hosts of the enemy may melt away, before
a blow is struck, at the very sight of the Crucified.
Still, as of old,

> "The Church's one Foundation
> Is Jesus Christ her Lord."

Still, as of old, she must labour, in all humility
but in all confidence; she must bear the burdens
of the weak, and bid the oppressor cease; she
must work and pray, alike for all sorts and
conditions of men,

> "Till with the vision glorious
> Her longing eyes are blest,
> And the great Church victorious
> Shall be the Church at rest."

PRINTED BY WILLIAM CLOWES AND SONS, LIMITED,
LONDON AND BECCLES.

A Catalogue of Works

IN

THEOLOGICAL LITERATURE

PUBLISHED BY

Messrs. LONGMANS, GREEN, & CO.

39 Paternoster Row, London, E.C.

Abbey and Overton.—THE ENGLISH CHURCH IN THE EIGHTEENTH CENTURY. By Charles J. Abbey, M.A., Rector of Checkendon, Reading, and John H. Overton, M.A., Rector of Epworth, Doncaster, Rural Dean of Isle of Axholme. *Crown 8vo.* 7s. 6d.

Adams.—SACRED ALLEGORIES. The Shadow of the Cross —The Distant Hills—The Old Man's Home—The King's Messengers. By the Rev. William Adams, M.A. *Crown 8vo.* 3s. 6d.

The Four Allegories may be had separately, with Illustrations. 16mo. 1s. each. *Also the Miniature Edition. Four Vols. 32mo.* 1s. each; in a box, 5s.

Aids to the Inner Life.

Edited by the Rev. W. H. Hutchings, M.A., Rector of Kirkby Misperton, Yorkshire. *Five Vols. 32mo, cloth limp, 6d. each; or cloth extra, 1s. each. Sold separately.*
Also an Edition *with red borders, 2s. each.*

OF THE IMITATION OF CHRIST. By Thomas à Kempis. In Four Books.

THE CHRISTIAN YEAR.

THE DEVOUT LIFE. By St. Francis de Sales.

THE HIDDEN LIFE OF THE SOUL. From the French of Jean Nicolas Grou.

THE SPIRITUAL COMBAT. By Lawrence Scupoli.

Bathe.—Works by the Rev. Anthony Bathe, M.A.

A LENT WITH JESUS. A Plain Guide for Churchmen. Containing Readings for Lent and Easter Week, and on the Holy Eucharist. 32mo, 1s.; *or in paper cover, 6d.*

WHAT I SHOULD BELIEVE. A Simple Manual of Self-Instruction for Church People. *Crown 8vo.* 3s. 6d.

Bickersteth.—Works by EDWARD HENRY BICKERSTETH, D.D., Bishop of Exeter.

THE LORD'S TABLE; or, Meditations on the Holy Communion Office in the Book of Common Prayer. 16mo. 1s.; *or cloth extra,* 2s.

YESTERDAY, TO-DAY, AND FOR EVER: a Poem in Twelve Books. *One Shilling Edition,* 18mo. *With red borders,* 16mo, 2s. 6d.
The Crown 8vo Edition (5s.) *may still be had.*

Blunt.—Works by the Rev. JOHN HENRY BLUNT, D.D.

THE ANNOTATED BOOK OF COMMON PRAYER: Being an Historical, Ritual, and Theological Commentary on the Devotional System of the Church of England. Edited by the Rev. JOHN HENRY BLUNT, D.D. 4to. 21s.

THE COMPENDIOUS EDITION OF THE ANNOTATED BOOK OF COMMON PRAYER: Forming a concise Commentary on the Devotional System of the Church of England. Edited by the Rev. JOHN HENRY BLUNT, D.D. *Crown 8vo.* 10s. 6d.

DICTIONARY OF DOCTRINAL AND HISTORICAL THEOLOGY. By various Writers. Edited by the Rev. JOHN HENRY BLUNT, D.D. *Imperial 8vo.* 21s.

DICTIONARY OF SECTS, HERESIES, ECCLESIASTICAL PARTIES AND SCHOOLS OF RELIGIOUS THOUGHT. By various Writers. Edited by the Rev. JOHN HENRY BLUNT, D.D. *Imperial 8vo.* 21s.

THE BOOK OF CHURCH LAW. Being an Exposition of the Legal Rights and Duties of the Parochial Clergy and the Laity of the Church of England. Revised by Sir WALTER G. F. PHILLIMORE, Bart., D.C.L. *Crown 8vo.* 7s. 6d.

A COMPANION TO THE BIBLE: Being a Plain Commentary on Scripture History, to the end of the Apostolic Age. *Two vols. small 8vo. Sold separately.*

THE OLD TESTAMENT. 3s. 6d.   THE NEW TESTAMENT. 3s. 6d.

HOUSEHOLD THEOLOGY: a Handbook of Religious Information respecting the Holy Bible, the Prayer Book, the Church, the Ministry, Divine Worship, the Creeds, etc. etc. *Paper cover,* 16mo. 1s. Also the Larger Edition, 3s. 6d.

Body.—Works by the Rev. GEORGE BODY, D.D., Canon of Durham.

THE SCHOOL OF CALVARY; or, Laws of Christian Life revealed from the Cross. A Course of Lectures delivered in substance at All Saints', Margaret Street. *Small 8vo.* 3s. 6d.

THE LIFE OF JUSTIFICATION: a Series of Lectures delivered in substance at All Saints', Margaret Street. 16mo. 2s. 6d.

THE LIFE OF TEMPTATION: a Course of Lectures delivered in substance at St. Peter's, Eaton Square; also at All Saints', Margaret Street. 16mo. 2s. 6d.

Boultbee.—A COMMENTARY ON THE THIRTY-NINE ARTICLES OF THE CHURCH OF ENGLAND. By the Rev. T. P. BOULTBEE, formerly Principal of the London College of Divinity, St. John's Hall, Highbury. *Crown 8vo.* 6s.

Bright.—Works by WILLIAM BRIGHT, D.D., Canon of Christ Church, Oxford.

LESSONS FROM THE LIVES OF THREE GREAT FATHERS: St. Athanasius, St. Chrysostom, and St. Augustine. *Crown 8vo.* 6s.

THE INCARNATION AS A MOTIVE POWER. *Crown 8vo.* 6s.

FAITH AND LIFE: Readings for the greater Holy Days, and the Sundays from Advent to Trinity. Compiled from Ancient Writers. *Small 8vo.* 5s.

IONA AND OTHER VERSES. *Small 8vo.* 4s. 6d.

HYMNS AND OTHER VERSES. *Small 8vo.* 5s.

Bright and Medd.—LIBER PRECUM PUBLICARUM ECCLESIÆ ANGLICANÆ. A GULIELMO BRIGHT, S.T.P., et PETRO GOLDSMITH MEDD, A.M., Latine redditus. [In hac Editione continentur Versiones Latinæ—1. Libri Precum Publicarum Ecclesiæ Anglicanæ ; 2. Liturgiæ Primæ Reformatæ ; 3. Liturgiæ Scoticanæ ; 4. Liturgiæ Americanæ.] *Small 8vo.* 7s. 6d.

Browne.—AN EXPOSITION OF THE THIRTY-NINE ARTICLES, Historical and Doctrinal. By E. H. BROWNE, D.D., formerly Bishop of Winchester. *8vo.* 16s.

Campion and Beamont.—THE PRAYER BOOK INTERLEAVED. With Historical Illustrations and Explanatory Notes arranged parallel to the Text. By W. M. CAMPION, D.D., and W. J. BEAMONT, M.A. *Small 8vo.* 7s. 6d.

Carter.—Works edited by the Rev. T. T. CARTER, M.A., Hon. Canon of Christ Church, Oxford.

THE TREASURY OF DEVOTION : a Manual of Prayer for General and Daily Use. Compiled by a Priest. *18mo.* 2s. 6d. ; *cloth limp,* 2s. ; *or bound with the Book of Common Prayer,* 3s. 6d. *Large-Type Edition. Crown 8vo.* 3s. 6d.

THE WAY OF LIFE : A Book of Prayers and Instruction for the Young at School, with a Preparation for Confirmation. Compiled by a Priest. *18mo.* 1s. 6d.

THE PATH OF HOLINESS : a First Book of Prayers, with the Service of the Holy Communion, for the Young. Compiled by a Priest. With Illustrations. *16mo.* 1s. 6d. ; *cloth limp,* 1s.

THE GUIDE TO HEAVEN : a Book of Prayers for every Want. (For the Working Classes.) Compiled by a Priest. *18mo.* 1s. 6d. ; *cloth limp,* 1s. *Large-Type Edition. Crown 8vo.* 1s. 6d. ; *cloth limp,* 1s.

[continued.

Oarter.—Works edited by the Rev. T. T. CARTER, M.A., Hon. Canon of Christ Church, Oxford—*continued.*

SELF-RENUNCIATION.   *16mo.*   *2s. 6d.*   *Also the Larger Edition. Small 8vo.*   *3s. 6d.*

THE STAR OF CHILDHOOD; a First Book of Prayers and Instruction for Children. Compiled by a Priest. With Illustrations. *16mo.* *2s. 6d.*

Oarter.—MAXIMS AND GLEANINGS FROM THE WRITINGS OF T. T. CARTER, M.A. Selected and arranged for Daily Use. *Crown 16mo.* *1s.*

Chandler.—THE SPIRIT OF MAN : An Essay in Christian Philosophy. By the Rev. A. CHANDLER, M.A., Rector of Poplar, E. *Crown 8vo.* *5s.*

Oonybeare and Howson.—THE LIFE AND EPISTLES OF ST. PAUL. By the Rev. W. J. CONYBEARE, M.A., and the Very Rev. J. S. HOWSON, D.D. With numerous Maps and Illustrations.

      LIBRARY EDITION. *Two Vols.* *8vo.* *21s.*
      STUDENT'S EDITION. *One Vol.* *Crown 8vo.* *6s.*

Orake.—HISTORY OF THE CHURCH UNDER THE ROMAN EMPIRE, A.D. 30-476. By the Rev. A. D. CRAKE, B.A. *Crown 8vo.* *7s. 6d.*

Devotional Series, 16mo, Red Borders. *Each 2s. 6d.*

BICKERSTETH'S YESTERDAY, TO-DAY, AND FOR EVER.
CHILCOT'S TREATISE ON EVIL THOUGHTS.
THE CHRISTIAN YEAR.
DEVOTIONAL BIRTHDAY BOOK.
HERBERT'S POEMS AND PROVERBS.
KEMPIS' (À) OF THE IMITATION OF CHRIST.
ST. FRANCIS DE SALES' THE DEVOUT LIFE.
WILSON'S THE LORD'S SUPPER. *Large type.*
*TAYLOR'S (JEREMY) HOLY LIVING.
* ⸺   ⸺   HOLY DYING.
      * *These two in one Volume.* *5s.*

Devotional Series, 18mo, without Red Borders. *Each 1s.*

BICKERSTETH'S YESTERDAY, TO-DAY, AND FOR EVER.
THE CHRISTIAN YEAR.
HERBERT'S POEMS AND PROVERBS.
KEMPIS' (À) OF THE IMITATION OF CHRIST.
ST. FRANCIS DE SALES' THE DEVOUT LIFE.
. WILSON'S THE LORD'S SUPPER. *Large type.*
*TAYLOR'S (JEREMY) HOLY LIVING.
* ⸺   ⸺   HOLY DYING.
      * *These two in one Volume.* *2s. 6d.*

Edersheim.—Works by ALFRED EDERSHEIM, M.A., D.D., Ph.D., sometime Grinfield Lecturer on the Septuagint, Oxford.

THE LIFE AND TIMES OF JESUS THE MESSIAH. *Two Vols.* 8*vo.* 24*s.*

JESUS THE MESSIAH : being an Abridged Edition of ' The Life and Times of Jesus the Messiah.' *Crown* 8*vo.* 7*s.* 6*d.*

PROPHECY AND HISTORY IN RELATION TO THE MESSIAH : The Warburton Lectures, 1880-1884. 8*vo.* 12*s.*

TOHU-VA-VOHU ('Without Form and Void'): being a collection of Fragmentary Thoughts and Criticism. *Crown* 8*vo.* 6*s.*

Ellicott.—Works by C. J. ELLICOTT, D.D., Bishop of Gloucester and Bristol.

A CRITICAL AND GRAMMATICAL COMMENTARY ON ST. PAUL'S EPISTLES. Greek Text, with a Critical and Grammatical Commentary, and a Revised English Translation. 8*vo.*

1 CORINTHIANS. 16*s.*

GALATIANS. 8*s.* 6*d.*

EPHESIANS. 8*s.* 6*d.*

PASTORAL EPISTLES. 10*s.* 6*d.*

PHILIPPIANS, COLOSSIANS, AND PHILEMON. 10*s.* 6*d.*

THESSALONIANS. 7*s.* 6*d.*

HISTORICAL LECTURES ON THE LIFE OF OUR LORD JESUS CHRIST. 8*vo.* 12*s.*

Epochs of Church History. Edited by MANDELL CREIGHTON, D.D., LL.D., Bishop of Peterborough. *Fcap.* 8*vo.* 2*s.* 6*d. each.*

THE ENGLISH CHURCH IN OTHER LANDS. By the Rev. H. W. TUCKER, M.A.

THE HISTORY OF THE RE-FORMATION IN ENGLAND. By the Rev. GEO. G. PERRY, M.A.

THE CHURCH OF THE EARLY FATHERS. By the Rev. ALFRED PLUMMER, D.D.

THE EVANGELICAL REVIVAL IN THE EIGHTEENTH CENTURY. By the Rev. J. H. OVERTON, M.A.

THE UNIVERSITY OF OXFORD. By the Hon. G. C. BRODRICK, D.C.L.

THE UNIVERSITY OF CAM-BRIDGE. By J. BASS MULLINGER, M.A.

THE ENGLISH CHURCH IN THE MIDDLE AGES. By the Rev. W. HUNT, M.A.

THE CHURCH AND THE EASTERN EMPIRE. By the Rev. H. F. TOZER, M.A.

THE CHURCH AND THE ROMAN EMPIRE. By the Rev. A. CARR.

THE CHURCH AND THE PURI-TANS, 1570-1660. By HENRY OFFLEY WAKEMAN, M.A.

HILDEBRAND AND HIS TIMES. By the Rev. W. R. W. STEPHENS, M.A.

THE POPES AND THE HOHEN-STAUFEN. By UGO BALZANI.

THE COUNTER-REFORMATION. By ADOLPHUS WILLIAM WARD, Litt. D.

WYCLIFFE AND MOVEMENTS FOR REFORM. By REGINALD L. POOLE, M.A.

THE ARIAN CONTROVERSY. By H. M. GWATKIN, M.A.

Fosbery.—Works edited by the Rev. THOMAS VINCENT FOSBERY, M.A., sometime Vicar of St. Giles's, Reading.

VOICES OF COMFORT. *Cheap Edition. Small 8vo.* 3*s.* 6*d.*
The Larger Edition (7*s.* 6*d.*) *may still be had.*

HYMNS AND POEMS FOR THE SICK AND SUFFERING. In connection with the Service for the Visitation of the Sick. Selected from Various Authors. *Small 8vo.* 3*s.* 6*d.*

Garland.—THE PRACTICAL TEACHING OF THE APO-CALYPSE. By the Rev. G. V. GARLAND, M.A. *8vo.* 16*s.*

Gore.—Works by the Rev. CHARLES GORE, M.A., Principal of the Pusey House ; Fellow of Trinity College, Oxford.

THE MINISTRY OF THE CHRISTIAN CHURCH. *8vo.* 10*s.* 6*d.*
ROMAN CATHOLIC CLAIMS. *Crown 8vo.* 3*s.* 6*d.*

Goulburn.—Works by EDWARD MEYRICK GOULBURN, D.D., D.C.L., sometime Dean of Norwich.

THOUGHTS ON PERSONAL RELIGION. *Small 8vo,* 6*s.* 6*d.* ; *Cheap Edition,* 3*s.* 6*d.* ; *Presentation Edition,* 2 *vols. small 8vo,* 10*s.* 6*d.*

THE PURSUIT OF HOLINESS : a Sequel to 'Thoughts on Personal Religion.' *Small 8vo.* 5*s. Cheap Edition,* 3*s.* 6*d.*

THE CHILD SAMUEL : a Practical and Devotional Commentary on the Birth and Childhood of the Prophet Samuel, as recorded in 1 Sam. i., ii. 1-27, iii. *Small 8vo.* 2*s.* 6*d.*

THE GOSPEL OF THE CHILDHOOD : a Practical and Devotional Commentary on the Single Incident of our Blessed Lord's Childhood (St. Luke ii. 41 to the end). *Crown 8vo.* 2*s.* 6*d.*

THE COLLECTS OF THE DAY : an Exposition, Critical and Devotional, of the Collects appointed at the Communion. With Preliminary Essays on their Structure, Sources, etc. 2 *vols. Crown 8vo.* 8*s. each.*

THOUGHTS UPON THE LITURGICAL GOSPELS for the Sundays, one for each day in the year. With an Introduction on their Origin, History, the Modifications made in them by the Reformers and by the Revisers of the Prayer Book. 2 *vols. Crown 8vo.* 16*s.*

MEDITATIONS UPON THE LITURGICAL GOSPELS for the Minor Festivals of Christ, the two first Week-days of the Easter and Whitsun Festivals, and the Red-letter Saints' Days. *Crown 8vo.* 8*s.* 6*d.*

FAMILY PRAYERS compiled from various sources (chiefly from Bishop Hamilton's Manual), and arranged on the Liturgical Principle. *Crown 8vo.* 3*s.* 6*d. Cheap Edition.* 16*mo.* 1*s.*

Harrison.—PROBLEMS OF CHRISTIANITY AND SCEPTI-CISM ; Lessons from Twenty Years' Experience in the Field of Christian Evidence. By the Rev. ALEXANDER J. HARRISON, B.D., Lecturer of the Christian Evidence Society. *Crown 8vo.* 7*s.* 6*d.*

Hernaman.—LYRA CONSOLATIONIS. From the Poets of the Seventeenth, Eighteenth, and Nineteenth Centuries. Selected and arranged by CLAUDIA FRANCES HERNAMAN. *Small 8vo. 6s.*

Holland.—Works by the Rev. HENRY SCOTT HOLLAND, M.A., Canon and Precentor of St. Paul's.

CREED AND CHARACTER : Sermons. *Crown 8vo. 7s. 6d.*

ON BEHALF OF BELIEF. Sermons preached in St. Paul's Cathedral. *Crown 8vo. 6s.*

CHRIST OR ECCLESIASTES. Sermons preached in St. Paul's Cathedral. *Crown 8vo. 3s. 6d.*

GOOD FRIDAY. Being Addresses on the Seven Last Words, delivered at St. Paul's Cathedral on Good Friday. *Small 8vo. 2s.*

LOGIC AND LIFE, with other Sermons. *Crown 8vo. 7s. 6d.*

Hopkins.—CHRIST THE CONSOLER. A Book of Comfort for the Sick. By ELLICE HOPKINS. *Small 8vo. 2s. 6d.*

Ingram.—HAPPINESS : In the Spiritual Life ; or, ' The Secret of the Lord.' A Series of Practical Considerations. By the Rev. W. CLAVELL INGRAM, M.A., Vicar of St. Matthew's, Leicester. *Crown 8vo. 7s. 6d.*

INHERITANCE, THE, OF THE SAINTS ; or, Thoughts on the Communion of Saints and the Life of the World to come. Collected chiefly from English Writers by L. P. With a Preface by the Rev. HENRY SCOTT HOLLAND, M.A. *Crown 8vo. 7s. 6d.*

Jameson.—Works by Mrs. JAMESON.

SACRED AND LEGENDARY ART, containing Legends of the Angels and Archangels, the Evangelists, the Apostles. With 19 etchings and 187 Woodcuts. *Two Vols. Cloth, gilt top, 20s. net.*

LEGENDS OF THE MONASTIC ORDERS, as represented in the Fine Arts. With 11 etchings and 88 Woodcuts. *One Vol. Cloth, gilt top, 10s. net.*

LEGENDS OF THE MADONNA, OR BLESSED VIRGIN MARY. With 27 Etchings and 165 Woodcuts. *One Vol. Cloth, gilt top, 10s. net.*

THE HISTORY OF OUR LORD, as exemplified in Works of Art. Commenced by the late Mrs. JAMESON ; continued and completed by LADY EASTLAKE. With 31 etchings and 281 Woodcuts. *Two Vols. 8vo. 20s. net.*

Jennings.—ECCLESIA ANGLICANA. A History of the Church of Christ in England from the Earliest to the Present Times. By the Rev. ARTHUR CHARLES JENNINGS, M.A. *Crown 8vo. 7s. 6d.*

Jukes.—Works by ANDREW JUKES.

THE NEW MAN AND THE ETERNAL LIFE. Notes on the Reiterated Amens of the Son of God. *Crown 8vo.* 6s.

THE NAMES OF GOD IN HOLY SCRIPTURE : a Revelation of His Nature and Relationships. *Crown 8vo.* 4s. 6d.

THE TYPES OF GENESIS. *Crown 8vo.* 7s. 6d.

THE SECOND DEATH AND THE RESTITUTION OF ALL THINGS. *Crown 8vo.* 3s. 6d.

THE MYSTERY OF THE KINGDOM. *Crown 8vo.* 2s. 6d.

Keble.—MAXIMS AND GLEANINGS FROM THE WRITINGS OF JOHN KEBLE, M.A. Selected and Arranged for Daily Use. By C. M. S. *Crown 16mo.* 1s.

SELECTIONS FROM THE WRITINGS OF JOHN KEBLE, M.A. *Crown 8vo.* 3s. 6d.

Kennaway.—CONSOLATIO ; OR, COMFORT FOR THE AFFLICTED. Edited by the late Rev. C. E. KENNAWAY. 16mo. 2s. 6d.

King.—DR. LIDDON'S TOUR IN EGYPT AND PALESTINE IN 1886. Being Letters descriptive of the Tour, written by his Sister, Mrs. KING. *Crown 8vo.* 5s.

Knox Little.—Works by W. J. KNOX LITTLE, M.A., Canon Residentiary of Worcester, and Vicar of Hoar Cross.

THE CHRISTIAN HOME. *Crown 8vo.* 6s. 6d.

THE HOPES AND DECISIONS OF THE PASSION OF OUR MOST HOLY REDEEMER. *Crown 8vo.* 3s. 6d.

THE THREE HOURS' AGONY OF OUR BLESSED REDEEMER. Being Addresses in the form of Meditations delivered in St. Alban's Church, Manchester, on Good Friday. *Small 8vo.* 2s. ; *or in Paper Cover,* 1s.

CHARACTERISTICS AND MOTIVES OF THE CHRISTIAN LIFE. Ten Sermons preached in Manchester Cathedral, in Lent and Advent. *Crown 8vo.* 3s. 6d.

SERMONS PREACHED FOR THE MOST PART IN MANCHESTER. *Crown 8vo.* 3s. 6d.

THE MYSTERY OF THE PASSION OF OUR MOST HOLY REDEEMER. *Crown 8vo.* 3s. 6d.

THE WITNESS OF THE PASSION OF OUR MOST HOLY REDEEMER. *Crown 8vo.* 3s. 6d.

THE LIGHT OF LIFE. Sermons preached on Various Occasions. *Crown 8vo.* 3s. 6d.

SUNLIGHT AND SHADOW IN THE CHRISTIAN LIFE. Sermons preached for the most part in America. *Crown 8vo.* 3s. 6d.

Lear.—Works by, and Edited by, H. L. SIDNEY LEAR.

> FOR DAYS AND YEARS. A Book containing a Text, Short Reading, and Hymn for Every Day in the Church's Year. 16mo. 2s. 6d. *Also a Cheap Edition*, 32mo. 1s.; *or cloth gilt*, 1s. 6d.
>
> FIVE MINUTES. Daily Readings of Poetry 16mo. 3s. 6d. *Also a Cheap Edition*. 32mo. 1s. ; *or cloth gilt*, 1s. 6d.
>
> WEARINESS. A Book for the Languid and Lonely. *Large Type. Small 8vo.* 5s.
>
> THE LIGHT OF THE CONSCIENCE. 16mo. 2s. 6d. 32mo. 1s.; *cloth limp*, 6d.
>
> CHRISTIAN BIOGRAPHIES. *Nine Vols. Crown 8vo.* 3s. 6d. *each.*

MADAME LOUISE DE FRANCE, Daughter of Louis XV., known also as the Mother Térèse de St. Augustin.

A DOMINICAN ARTIST: a Sketch of the Life of the Rev. Père Besson, of the Order of St. Dominic.

HENRI PERREYVE. By A. GRATRY.

ST. FRANCIS DE SALES, Bishop and Prince of Geneva.

THE REVIVAL OF PRIESTLY LIFE IN THE SEVENTEENTH CENTURY IN FRANCE.

A CHRISTIAN PAINTER OF THE NINETEENTH CENTURY.

BOSSUET AND HIS CONTEMPORARIES.

FÉNELON, ARCHBISHOP OF CAMBRAI.

HENRI DOMINIQUE LACORDAIRE.

DEVOTIONAL WORKS. Edited by H. L. SIDNEY LEAR. *New and Uniform Editions. Nine Vols.* 16mo. 2s. 6d. *each.*

FÉNELON'S SPIRITUAL LETTERS TO MEN.

FÉNELON'S SPIRITUAL LETTERS TO WOMEN.

A SELECTION FROM THE SPIRITUAL LETTERS OF ST. FRANCIS DE SALES.

THE SPIRIT OF ST. FRANCIS DE SALES.

THE HIDDEN LIFE OF THE SOUL.

THE LIGHT OF THE CONSCIENCE.

SELF-RENUNCIATION. From the French.

ST. FRANCIS DE SALES' OF THE LOVE OF GOD.

SELECTIONS FROM PASCAL'S THOUGHTS.

Library of Spiritual Works for English Catholics. *Original Edition. With Red Borders. Small 8vo.* 5s. *each. New and Cheaper Editions.* 16mo. 2s. 6d. *each.*

OF THE IMITATION OF CHRIST.

THE SPIRITUAL COMBAT. By LAURENCE SCUPOLI.

THE DEVOUT LIFE. By ST. FRANCIS DE SALES.

OF THE LOVE OF GOD. By ST. FRANCIS DE SALES.

THE CONFESSIONS OF ST. AUGUSTINE. *In Ten Books.*

THE CHRISTIAN YEAR. 5s *Edition only*

Liddon.—Works by HENRY PARRY LIDDON, D.D., D.C.L., LL.D., late Canon Residentiary and Chancellor of St. Paul's.

SERMONS ON OLD TESTAMENT SUBJECTS. *Crown 8vo.* 5s.

SERMONS ON SOME WORDS OF CHRIST. *Crown 8vo.*

THE DIVINITY OF OUR LORD AND SAVIOUR JESUS CHRIST. Being the Bampton Lectures for 1866. *Crown 8vo.* 5s.

ADVENT IN ST. PAUL'S. Sermons bearing chiefly on the Two Comings of our Lord. *Two Vols. Crown 8vo.* 3s. 6d. each. *Cheap Edition in one Volume. Crown 8vo.* 5s.

CHRISTMASTIDE IN ST. PAUL'S. Sermons bearing chiefly on the Birth of our Lord and the End of the Year. *Crown 8vo.* 5s.

PASSIONTIDE SERMONS. *Crown 8vo.* 5s.

EASTER IN ST. PAUL'S. Sermons bearing chiefly on the Resurrection of our Lord. *Two Vols. Crown 8vo.* 3s. 6d. each. *Cheap Edition in one Volume. Crown 8vo.* 5s.

SERMONS PREACHED BEFORE THE UNIVERSITY OF OXFORD. *Two Vols. Crown 8vo.* 3s. 6d. each. *Cheap Edition in one Volume. Crown 8vo.* 5s.

THE MAGNIFICAT. Sermons in St. Paul's. *Crown 8vo.* 2s. 6d.

SOME ELEMENTS OF RELIGION. Lent Lectures. *Small 8vo.* 2s. 6d. ; *or in Paper Cover,* 1s. 6d.

The Crown 8vo Edition (5s.) may still be had.

SELECTIONS FROM THE WRITINGS OF H. P. LIDDON, D.D. *Crown 8vo.* 3s. 6d.

MAXIMS AND GLEANINGS FROM THE WRITINGS OF H. P. LIDDON, D.D. Selected and arranged by C. M. S. *Crown 16mo.* 1s.

DR. LIDDON'S TOUR IN EGYPT AND PALESTINE IN 1886. Being Letters descriptive of the Tour, written by his Sister, Mrs. KING. *Crown 8vo.* 5s.

Luckock.—Works by HERBERT MORTIMER LUCKOCK, D.D., Canon of Ely.

AFTER DEATH. An Examination of the Testimony of Primitive Times respecting the State of the Faithful Dead, and their Relationship to the Living. *Crown 8vo.* 6s.

THE INTERMEDIATE STATE BETWEEN DEATH AND JUDGMENT. Being a Sequel to *After Death. Crown 8vo.* 6s.

FOOTPRINTS OF THE SON OF MAN, as traced by St. Mark. Being Eighty Portions for Private Study, Family Reading, and Instructions in Church. *Two Vols. Crown 8vo.* 12s. *Cheap Edition in one Vol. Crown 8vo.* 5s.

[*continued.*

Luckock.—Works by HERBERT MORTIMER LUCKOCK, D.D., Canon of Ely—*continued.*

THE DIVINE LITURGY. Being the Order for Holy Communion, Historically, Doctrinally, and Devotionally set forth, in Fifty Portions. *Crown 8vo.* 6s.

STUDIES IN THE HISTORY OF THE BOOK OF COMMON PRAYER. The Anglican Reform—The Puritan Innovations—The Elizabethan Reaction—The Caroline Settlement. With Appendices. *Crown 8vo.* 6s.

THE BISHOPS IN THE TOWER. A Record of Stirring Events affecting the Church and Nonconformists from the Restoration to the Revolution. *Crown 8vo.* 6s.

LYRA APOSTOLICA. Poems by J. W. BOWDEN, R. H. FROUDE, J. KEBLE, J. H. NEWMAN, R. I. WILBERFORCE, and I. WILLIAMS; and a New Preface by CARDINAL NEWMAN. 16mo. *With Red Borders.* 2s. 6d.

LYRA GERMANICA. Hymns translated from the German by CATHERINE WINKWORTH. *Small 8vo.* 5s.

MacColl.—CHRISTIANITY IN RELATION TO SCIENCE AND MORALS. By the Rev. MALCOLM MACCOLL, M.A., Canon Residentiary of Ripon. *Crown 8vo.* 6s.

Mason.—Works by A. J. MASON, D.D., formerly Fellow of Trinity College, Cambridge.

THE FAITH OF THE GOSPEL. A Manual of Christian Doctrine. *Crown 8vo.* 7s. 6d. *Also a Large-Paper Edition for Marginal Notes.* 4to. 12s. 6d.

THE RELATION OF CONFIRMATION TO BAPTISM. As taught in Holy Scripture and the Fathers. *Crown 8vo.* 7s. 6d.

Mercier.—OUR MOTHER CHURCH: Being Simple Talk on High Topics. By Mrs. JEROME MERCIER. *Small 8vo.* 3s. 6d.

Moberly.—Works by GEORGE MOBERLY, D.C.L., late Bishop of Salisbury.

PLAIN SERMONS. Preached at Brighstone. *Crown 8vo.* 5s.

THE SAYINGS OF THE GREAT FORTY DAYS, between the Resurrection and Ascension, regarded as the Outlines of the Kingdom of God. In Five Discourses. *Crown 8vo.* 5s.

PAROCHIAL SERMONS. Mostly preached at Brighstone. *Crown 8vo.* 7s. 6d.

SERMONS PREACHED AT WINCHESTER COLLEGE. *Two Vols. Small 8vo.* 6s. 6d. each. *Sold separately.*

Mozley.—Works by J. B. MOZLEY, D.D., late Canon of Christ Church, and Regius Professor of Divinity at Oxford.

ESSAYS, HISTORICAL AND THEOLOGICAL. *Two Vols. 8vo. 24s.*

EIGHT LECTURES ON MIRACLES. Being the Bampton Lectures for 1865. *Crown 8vo. 7s. 6d.*

RULING IDEAS IN EARLY AGES AND THEIR RELATION TO OLD TESTAMENT FAITH. Lectures delivered to Graduates of the University of Oxford. *8vo. 10s. 6d.*

SERMONS PREACHED BEFORE THE UNIVERSITY OF OXFORD, and on Various Occasions. *Crown 8vo. 7s. 6d.*

SERMONS, PAROCHIAL AND OCCASIONAL. *Crown 8vo. 7s. 6d.*

Mozley.—Works by the Rev. T. MOZLEY, M.A., Author of 'Reminiscences of Oriel College and the Oxford Movement.'

THE WORD. *Crown 8vo. 7s. 6d.*

THE SON. *Crown 8vo. 7s. 6d.*

LETTERS FROM ROME ON THE OCCASION OF THE ŒCUMENICAL COUNCIL 1869-1870. *Two Vols. Cr. 8vo. 18s.*

Newbolt.—Works by the Rev. W. C. E. NEWBOLT, M.A., Canon Residentiary of St. Paul's.

THE FRUIT OF THE SPIRIT. Being Ten Addresses bearing on the Spiritual Life. *Crown 8vo. 2s. 6d.*

THE MAN OF GOD. Being Six Addresses delivered during Lent 1886, at the Primary Ordination of the Right Rev. the Lord Alwyne Compton, D.D., Bishop of Ely. *Small 8vo. 1s. 6d.*

THE VOICE OF THE PRAYER BOOK. Being Spiritual Addresses bearing on the Book of Common Prayer. *Crown 8vo. 2s. 6d.*

Newnham.—THE ALL-FATHER : Sermons preached in a Village Church. By the Rev. H. P. NEWNHAM. With Preface by EDNA LYALL. *Crown 8vo. 4s. 6d.*

Newnham.—ALRESFORD ESSAYS FOR THE TIMES. By Rev. W. O. NEWNHAM, M.A., late Rector of Alresford. CONTENTS :— Bible Story of Creation—Bible Story of Eden—Bible Story of the Deluge—After Death—Miracles : A Conversation—Eternal Punishment —The Resurrection of the Body. *Crown 8vo. 6s.*

Newman.—Works by JOHN ¡HENRY NEWMAN, B.D., sometime Vicar of St. Mary's, Oxford.

PAROCHIAL AND PLAIN SERMONS. *Eight Vols. Cabinet Edition. Crown 8vo. 5s. each. Popular Edition. Eight Vols. Crown 8vo. 3s. 6d. each.*

SELECTION, ADAPTED TO THE SEASONS OF THE ECCLE-SIASTICAL YEAR, from the 'Parochial and Plain Sermons.' *Cabinet Edition. Crown 8vo. 5s. Popular Edition. Crown 8vo. 3s. 6d.* .

FIFTEEN SERMONS PREACHED BEFORE THE UNIVERSITY OF OXFORD, between A.D. 1826 and 1843. *Crown 8vo. 5s.*

SERMONS BEARING UPON SUBJECTS OF THE DAY. *Cabinet Edition. Crown 8vo. 5s. Popular Edition. Crown 8vo. 3s. 6d.*

LECTURES ON THE DOCTRINE OF JUSTIFICATION. *Crown 8vo. 5s.* .

THE LETTERS AND CORRESPONDENCE OF JOHN HENRY NEWMAN DURING HIS LIFE IN THE ENGLISH CHURCH. With a Brief Autobiographical Memoir. Arranged and Edited by ANNE MOZLEY. *Two Vols. 8vo. 30s. net.*

** For other Works by Cardinal Newman, see Messrs. Longmans & Co.'s Catalogue of Works in General Literature.

Csborne.—Works by EDWARD OSBORNE, Mission Priest of the Society of St. John the Evangelist, Cowley, Oxford.

THE CHILDREN'S SAVIOUR. Instructions to Children on the Life of our Lord and Saviour Jesus Christ. *Illustrated. 16mo. 2s. 6d.*

THE SAVIOUR-KING. Instructions to Children on Old Testament Types and Illustrations of the Life of Christ. *Illustrated. 16mo. 2s. 6d.*

THE CHILDREN'S FAITH. Instructions to Children on the Apostles' Creed. *Illustrated. 16mo. 2s. 6d.*

Oxenden.—Works by the Right Rev. ASHTON OXENDEN, formerly Bishop of Montreal.

THE HISTORY OF MY LIFE : An Autobiography. *Crown 8vo. 5s.*

PEACE AND ITS HINDRANCES. *Crown 8vo. 1s. ; sewed, 2s., cloth.*

THE PATHWAY OF SAFETY ; or, Counsel to the Awakened. *Fcap. 8vo, large type. 2s. 6d. Cheap Edition. Small type, limp. 1s.*

THE EARNEST COMMUNICANT. *New Red Rubric Edition. 32mo, cloth. 2s. Common Edition. 32mo, 1s.*

OUR CHURCH AND HER SERVICES. *Fcap. 8vo. 2s. 6d.*

[*continued.*

Oxenden.—Works by the Right Rev. ASHTON OXENDEN, formerly Bishop of Montreal—*continued.*

FAMILY PRAYERS FOR FOUR WEEKS. First Series. *Fcap. 8vo.* 2s. 6d. Second Series. *Fcap. 8vo.* 2s. 6d.
LARGE TYPE EDITION. Two Series in one Volume. *Crown 8vo.* 6s.

COTTAGE SERMONS; or, Plain Words to the Poor. *Fcap. 8vo.* 2s. 6d.

THOUGHTS FOR HOLY WEEK. *16mo, cloth.* 1s. 6d.

DECISION. *18mo.* 1s. 6d.

THE HOME BEYOND ; or, A Happy Old Age. *Fcap. 8vo.* 1s. 6d.

THE LABOURING MAN'S BOOK. *18mo, large type, cloth.* 1s. 6d.

Paget.—Works by FRANCIS PAGET, D.D., Dean of Christ Church, Oxford.

THE SPIRIT OF DISCIPLINE : Sermons. *Crown 8vo.* 6s. 6d.

FACULTIES AND DIFFICULTIES FOR BELIEF AND DIS-BELIEF. *Crown 8vo.* 6s. 6d.

THE HALLOWING OF WORK. Addresses given at Eton, January 16-18, 1888. *Small 8vo.* 2s.

PRACTICAL REFLECTIONS. By a CLERGYMAN. With Prefaces by H. P. LIDDON, D.D., D.C.L. *Crown 8vo.*

Vol. I.—THE HOLY GOSPELS. 4s. 6d.

Vol. II.—ACTS TO REVELATION. 6s.

THE PSALMS. 5s.

PRIEST (THE) TO THE ALTAR ; Or, Aids to the Devout Celebration of Holy Communion, chiefly after the Ancient English Use of Sarum. *Royal 8vo.* 12s.

Pusey.—Works by E. B. PUSEY, D.D.

PRIVATE PRAYERS. With Preface by H. P. LIDDON, D.D. *32mo.* 1s.

PRAYERS FOR A YOUNG SCHOOLBOY. With a Preface by H. P. LIDDON, D.D. *24mo.* 1s.

SELECTIONS FROM THE WRITINGS OF EDWARD BOUVERIE PUSEY, D.D. *Crown 8vo.* 3s. 6d.

MAXIMS AND GLEANINGS FROM THE WRITINGS OF EDWARD BOUVERIE PUSEY, D.D. Selected and Arranged for Daily Use. By C. M. S. *Crown 16mo.* 1s.

Reynolds.—THE NATURAL HISTORY OF IMMORTALITY. By the Rev. J. W. REYNOLDS, M.A., Prebendary of St. Paul's. *Crown 8vo.* 7s. 6d.

Richmond.—CHRISTIAN ECONOMICS. By the Rev. WILFRID RICHMOND, M.A., sometime Warden of Trinity College, Glenalmond. *Crown 8vo.* 6*s.*

Sanday.—THE ORACLES OF GOD : Nine Lectures on the Nature and Extent of Biblical Inspiration and the Special Significance of the Old Testament Scriptures at the Present Time. By W. SANDAY, M.A., D.D., LL.D., Dean Ireland's Professor of Exegesis and Fellow of Exeter College. *Crown 8vo.* 4*s.*

Seebohm.—THE OXFORD REFORMERS—JOHN COLET, ERASMUS, AND THOMAS MORE : A History of their Fellow-Work. By FREDERIC SEEBOHM. 8*vo.* 14*s.*

Stanton.—THE PLACE OF AUTHORITY IN MATTERS OF RELIGIOUS BELIEF. By VINCENT HENRY STANTON, D.D., Fellow of Trinity College, Ely Professor of Divinity, Cambridge. *Crown 8vo.* 6*s.*

Stephen.—ESSAYS IN ECCLESIASTICAL BIOGRAPHY. By the Right Hon. Sir J. STEPHEN. *Crown 8vo.* 7*s.* 6*d.*

Swayne.—THE BLESSED DEAD IN PARADISE. Four All Saints' Day Sermons, preached in Salisbury Cathedral. By R. G. SWAYNE, M.A. *Crown 8vo.* 3*s.* 6*d.*

Tweddell.—THE SOUL IN CONFLICT. A Practical Examination of some Difficulties and Duties of the Spiritual Life. By MARSHALL TWEDDELL, M.A., Vicar of St. Saviour, Paddington. *Crown 8vo.* 6*s.*

Twells.—COLLOQUIES ON PREACHING. By HENRY TWELLS, M.A., Honorary Canon of Peterborough. *Crown 8vo.* 5*s.*

Wakeman.—THE HISTORY OF RELIGION IN ENGLAND. By HENRY OFFLEY WAKEMAN, M.A. *Small 8vo.* 1*s.* 6*d.*

Welldon. — THE FUTURE AND THE PAST. Sermons preached to Harrow Boys. By the Rev. J. E. C. WELLDON, M.A., Head Master of Harrow School. *Crown 8vo.* 7*s.* 6*d.*

Williams.—Works by the Rev. ISAAC WILLIAMS, B.D.

A DEVOTIONAL COMMENTARY ON THE GOSPEL NARRATIVE. *Eight Vols. Crown 8vo.* 5*s. each. Sold separately.*

THOUGHTS ON THE STUDY OF THE HOLY GOSPELS.

A HARMONY OF THE FOUR GOSPELS.

OUR LORD'S NATIVITY.

OUR LORD'S MINISTRY (Second Year).

OUR LORD'S MINISTRY (Third Year).

THE HOLY WEEK.

OUR LORD'S PASSION.

OUR LORD'S RESURRECTION.

FEMALE CHARACTERS OF HOLY SCRIPTURE. A Series of Sermons. *Crown 8vo.* 5*s.*

[*continued.*

Williams.—Works by the Rev. ISAAC WILLIAMS, B.D., formerly Fellow of Trinity College, Oxford—*continued.*

THE CHARACTERS OF THE OLD TESTAMENT. A Series of Sermons. *Crown 8vo.* 5s.

THE APOCALYPSE. With Notes and Reflections. *Crown 8vo.* 5s.

SERMONS ON THE EPISTLES AND GOSPELS FOR THE SUNDAYS AND HOLY DAYS THROUGHOUT THE YEAR. *Two Vols. Crown 8vo.* 5s. *each.*

PLAIN SERMONS ON THE CATECHISM. *Two Vols. Crown 8vo.* 5s. *each.*

SELECTIONS FROM THE WRITINGS OF ISAAC WILLIAMS, B.D. *Crown 8vo.* 3s. 6d.

Woodford.—Works by JAMES RUSSELL WOODFORD, D.D., sometime Lord Bishop of Ely.

THE GREAT COMMISSION. Twelve Addresses on the Ordinal. Edited, with an Introduction on the Ordinations of his Episcopate, by HERBERT MORTIMER LUCKOCK, D.D. *Crown 8vo.* 5s.

SERMONS ON OLD AND NEW TESTAMENT SUBJECTS. Edited by HERBERT MORTIMER LUCKOCK, D.D. *Crown 8vo.* 5s.

Woodruff. — THE CHILDREN'S YEAR. Verses for the Sundays and Holy Days throughout the Year. By C. H. WOODRUFF, B.C.L. With an Introduction by the LORD BISHOP OF SOUTHWELL. *Fcap. 8vo.* 3s. 6d.

Wordsworth.

For List of Works by the late Christopher Wordsworth, D.D., Bishop of Lincoln, see Messrs. Longmans & Co.'s Catalogue of Theological Works, 32 pp. Sent post free on application.

Wordsworth.—Works by ELIZABETH WORDSWORTH, Principal of Lady Margaret Hall, Oxford.

ILLUSTRATIONS OF THE CREED. *Crown 8vo.* 5s.

CHRISTOPHER AND OTHER POEMS. *Crown 8vo.* 6s.

Younghusband.—Works by FRANCES YOUNGHUSBAND.

THE STORY OF OUR LORD, told in Simple Language for Children. With 25 Illustrations from Pictures by the Old Masters. *Crown 8vo.* 2s. 6d.

THE STORY OF GENESIS, told in Simple Language for Children. *Crown 8vo.* 2s. 6d.

THE STORY OF THE EXODUS, told in Simple Language for Children. With Map and 29 Illustrations. *Crown 8vo.* 2s. 6d.

Printed by T. and A. CONSTABLE, Printers to Her Majesty, *at the Edinburgh University Press.*

20,000/12/91.